S0-DGM-095

Theology Today

GENERAL EDITOR

EDWARD YARNOLD, S.J.

No. 33

The Priest as Preacher Past and Future

BY

EDWARD P. ECHLIN, S.J.

FIDES PUBLISHERS, INC.

NOTRE DAME, INDIANA

Dedication – to Bruce, Don, Michael, Stephen, Kevin and Brian.

ACKNOWLEDGEMENTS

The Scripture quotations in this publication are from the Revised Standard Version of the Bible, copyrighted 1946 and 1952 by the Division of Christian Education of the National Council of the Churches of Christ in the U.S.A. and used by kind permission. Quotations from *The Documents of Vatican II* (ed. W. M. Abbott, S.J.) are printed by kind permission of The America Press and Geoffrey Chapman Ltd., London. Thanks are also due to S.P.C.K. for permission to quote from Don Gregory Dix's edition of the *Apostolic Tradition* and from *The Ordination Prayers of the Ancient Western Churches*.

ABBREVIATIONS

PL J.P. Migne: *Patrologia Latina*
CIC *Codex Iuris Canonici*

CONTENTS

PREFACE

In these days many priests feel the need to question the nature of the priesthood. Are their functions primarily liturgical, centred on the Mass, or pastoral, consisting of visiting, teaching, counselling? Fr Echlin investigates the origins of the Christian priesthood and reaches the conclusion that the priest is above all a preacher. This role, in fact, includes all others; for example, to offer the Mass is to 'proclaim the Lord's death' (1 Cor 11.26), and to forgive sins is to receive the sinner back into the community of those who hear and accept God's word.

Another fact emerges in the course of the book: the flexibility of the structure of the early Church. For example, in some places 'prophets' presided at the Eucharist. Again, it was not until the second century that the rule of one bishop to a see became normal. Schemas for reunion between Churches must not be frustrated through the misconception that the present hierarchical pattern in the Catholic Church is the only one possible.

E. J. Yarnold, S.J.

INTRODUCTION

According to Vatican II priests 'as co-workers with their bishops, have the primary duty of proclaiming the word of God to all.' It is not surprising therefore that in the renewal of Catholic ministry now under way preaching is a pressing theological question.

With the emergence of educated laymen seeking ultimate meaning in industrialized societies dissatisfaction with ministerial preaching has reached serious proportions. Young and old, progressive and traditionalist, rich and poor – within all these groups there is a demand for better preaching than has been experienced. This yearning of God's people for more and better preaching may well be the voice of the Spirit. It may in fact be the prompting of the Spirit to lead the Church out of its present crisis in the ministry.

It is my conviction that there is a convergence in the laity's demand for informed preaching and the priest's search for identity. Identity is the role assigned to a man in a community, the role expected of him, the role from which he derives his life-giving realization of personal value. The priest may find his identity by responding to the yearning of God's people for better informed preaching.

The renewal of preaching is more than a structural adaptation to meet contemporary yearnings. Preaching is central to the very reality of a Christian ministry. Within the historic reality of the ministry the presbyter-priest as co-operator with the episcopal order has since ancient times been the foremost servant of the world in a local community. He is the primary preacher in the local Church; and preaching is his primary service.

For Christianity is the response to God's self-disclosure in Christ. Christ's mission of human and cosmic reconciliation continues today in the people of God. And reconciliation begins and continues with the preaching of the gospel. Without preaching there would be no community, no cult, no shepherds, no reconciliation.

The primary duty of the priest is to proclaim the gospel even to lost sheep, to unite the believing community, to lead them to the Eucharist, and to guide the community in its mission of bringing eucharistic reconciliation to the world.

The priest as preacher will find his identity in continuity with the priest of the past. Without a sense of history and continuity with his past no man can understand who he is or where he is heading. This book attempts to illuminate the preaching ministry of today by surveying the past priest as preacher. The preaching office of the first servants of the word gradually funnelled into that of this bishop and his presbyterate. With the proliferation of local parishes the presbyter-priest served as primary preacher in the local Church. In the middle ages there was a decline in preaching and the subsequent rise and decline of the preaching friars. Preaching was a battlecry of the reformers and an issue at Trent and Vatican II. Some familiarity with the biography of the priest as preacher will illuminate the constants in the priest's preaching office and will provide wisdom for avoiding the pitfalls that ensnared our ancestors.

This book looks to the past not for the past's sake but with an eye to the future of the priest as preacher, a future in which the priest will recover his identity – as informed minister of the word – by responding to the yearnings of his people for better preaching. In the preface to his *Ecclesiastical History* Venerable Bede expressed to King Ceolwulf the relevance of historical continuity. His words express the purpose of this volume.

> If history records good things of good men, the thoughtful hearer is encouraged to imitate what is good; or if it records evil of wicked men, the devout, religious reader is encouraged to avoid all that is sinful and perverse and to follow what he knows to be good and pleasing to God.

CHAPTER I

THE ORIGINS OF CHRISTIAN PREACHING

In this chapter we shall view briefly some of the first Christian preachers whose service of the word eventually devolved upon the Christian priests of later centuries.

According to the New Testament *all* baptized Christians were to *preach* the good news. The first letter of Peter, possibly reflecting a primitive baptismal liturgy, includes proclamation as an office of the baptismal priesthood. 'You are a chosen race, a royal priesthood, a holy nation, God's own people, that you may declare the wonderful deeds of him who called you out of darkness into his marvellous light' (1 Pet 2.9; cf. Exod 19.5). Christians, united in faith and baptism to Christ the one mediator, share in his unique mediation.

Because preaching in a wide sense is a comprehensive ministry it takes a variety of forms which allow each Christian to preach according to his own gifts (1 Cor 14.26). The preaching of *all* Christians builds up the Church. Paul was able to say to the Thessalonians, 'Your faith has gone forth everywhere, so that we need not say anything' (1 Thess 1.8). Hans Küng describes well the preaching function of all Christians.

Every believer can and must, having been taught by God, teach others; can and must, having received the word of God, be its herald in some form or other. Every Christian is called to be a preacher of the word, in the widest sense, even though, in view of the variety of the gifts of the Spirit, not everyone can by any means do everything. All are called to preach the gospel in the sense of their personal Christian witness, without being all called to preach in the narrow sense of the word or to be theologians (Hans Küng, *The Church*, N.Y. 1967, p. 77).

An *official* Christian priesthood within this universal priesthood is an authentic development if Christian priests are dedicated preachers – especially but not exclusively of the spoken word.

We repeat that our aim in this chapter is to view the special ministers of the word within the universal priesthood whose service of preaching was eventually absorbed by presbyter-priests. Within a developed Christian ministry the focus of our concern will be the presbyters, the priests 'of the second grade', the servants of the word who for weal or for woe have today the central responsibility for the continuing education of God's People in the residential Churches. The development of the presbyter's preaching role is conjoined to the development of the bishop's — but at this moment in history it is the priest who is in the front lines and who is, therefore, our paramount concern.

The Apostles

The pre-eminent Christian preachers were and are the apostles (Eph 2.4). On the apostolic preaching all subsequent preaching is founded. The apostles, as the foundation of the Church, were unique. The apostles are those disciples who were commissioned by the risen Lord to preach in his name. Their apostleship and their preaching were of one piece. '...He who had set me apart before I was born, and had called me through his grace, was pleased to reveal his Son to me, in order that I might preach him among the Gentiles' (Gal 1.15-16). The apostles, like all Christian preachers, act in the name of the risen Christ. Christ risen is the key and the heart of their preaching. 'This Jesus God raised up and of that we are all witnesses' (Acts 2.27). The apostles — those commissioned by the risen Lord — included, in addition to the twelve, Paul, James, Barnabas, the Lord's brothers, and other apostles (1 Cor 12.8; Rom 12.8).

The Twelve

But the twelve were the apostles who were with Christ from the baptism by John the Baptist. They especially were preservers of the tradition about the earthly Jesus who died and rose from the dead — and for the twelve, no less than for other apostles, the resurrection was the focus of Christian preaching (Acts 2.32). The idea of 'the twelve' is not merely a post-resurrection development. For the twelve disciples, because they were with Jesus from the beginning of his public life, were unique (Lk 22.30); the twelve were an eschatological sign of the renewed and true Israel, they were the foundation stones of the New Jerusalem (Apoc 2.14). The twelve were to have a primary role in the final consummation of God's reign (Mt 19.28). And of great importance, they were acknowledged by the missionary apostle Paul as 'those who were apostles before me' (Gal 1.17).

The twelve were commissioned by the risen Lord to preach, teach, and baptize – to witness to the gospel to the ends of the earth (Mt 28.18; Acts 1.8). Except for Peter, and to a lesser extent John, there is little verifiable evidence that the twelve were actually missionary preachers. Yet at the mother Church of Jerusalem there is abundant testimony to their preaching. In fact the twelve refused to cease their preaching of the risen Christ when so commanded by Jewish authorities.

> And the high priest questioned them, saying, 'We strictly charged you not to teach in this name, yet here you have filled Jerusalem with your teaching and you intend to bring this man's blood upon us'. But Peter and the apostles answered, 'We must obey God rather than man' (Acts 5.27-29; cf. 4.20).

The twelve disciples who were with Jesus 'from the beginning' were, after Pentecost, a respected inner circle at Jerusalem who were concerned with the whole Church. As such they devoted themselves to preaching in Judea and to important decisions affecting Christian communities elsewhere. Two significant texts in Acts illustrate the preaching role of the twelve which has funnelled into the Christian priesthood.

The first important text is the Lukan description of the appointment of seven men, probably Hellenist leaders or presbyters, to minister to the daily needs of Hellenist widows. According to Luke the twelve considered their own prayerful ministry of the word so important that they declined to engage in social work.

> Now in these days when the disciples were increasing in number, the Hellenists murmured against the Hebrews because their widows were neglected in the daily distribution. And the twelve summoned the body of the disciples and said, 'It is not right that we should give up preaching the word of God to serve tables. Therefore, brethren, pick out from among you seven men of good repute, full of the Spirit and of wisdom,

whom we may appoint to this duty. But we will devote ourselves to prayer and to the ministry of the word.' And what they said pleased the whole multitude, and they chose Stephen, a man full of faith and of the Holy Spirit, and Philip, and Prochorus, and Nicanor, and Timon, and Parmenas, and Nicolaus, a proselyte of Antioch. These they set before the apostles, and they prayed and laid their hands upon them (Acts 6.1-6).

It is significant that the seven too were more engaged in spoken ministry of the word than in service at tables. At least two of them, Stephen and Philip (Acts 6.7f., 7.5, 35), preached the gospel. There is no evidence that the seven specialized in social work.

A second important text for the preaching role of the twelve, which was soon absorbed by Christian priests, – and here we mean preaching in the wide sense – is the account in Acts of the Jerusalem council which determined the fate of gentiles in the Church. The twelve appear as teachers, guides and interpreters, as ministers of the word through leadership. Parenthetically this passage, at least indirectly, has something to teach about the response of Christian preaching to the cancer of racism. The twelve, together with James, the presbyters, and the whole community, assembled to decide whether or not gentiles were to be circumcised before admission to the community. Peter spoke on behalf of the twelve – and his words carried the day.

Now therefore why do you make trial of God by putting a yoke upon the neck of the disciples which neither our fathers nor we have been able to bear? But we believe that we shall be saved through the grace of the Lord Jesus, just as they will (Acts 15.10-11).

Peter, the spokesman of the twelve, deserves special attention, not precisely because his pre-eminence among the twelve was later combined with the Roman bishopric, but because his preaching role has funnelled into the priesthood as well as into the episcopacy and papacy. Peter left Jerusalem to preach Christ in Antioch and Rome. The focus of his preaching was the resurrection as fulfilment of Jewish expectations (Acts 1.15.; 2.5f.; 3.18f.; 10.43). As first witness of the risen Christ, Peter strengthened his brethren through his preaching (1 Cor 15; Lk 22.32). As forerunner of all subsequent preachers, Peter instructed converts before baptism (Acts 2.8). As we have noticed, Peter preached that

14

Christianity embraced *all* men, and in welcoming the Roman official Cornelius to the Church Peter was instrumental in opening the community to *all* their neighbours. His preaching convinced many Jewish Christians that gentiles too were redeemed by the risen Christ.

'If then God gave the same gift to them as he gave to us when we believed in the Lord Jesus Christ, who was I that I could withstand God?' When they heard this they were silenced. And they glorified God, saying, 'Then to the Gentiles also God has granted repentance unto life' (Acts 11.17-18).

As first witness to the resurrection and first preacher among the twelve Peter's preaching was the foundation of the Church (Mt 16.16f.; cf. 18.18). Finally, Peter was a shepherd of the Christian flock, a symbol which, as we shall see, is rich in connotations of preaching the gospel (Jn 21.15-17).

Paul

The apostle about whom we know the most – and whose function of preaching has devolved upon today's priests – is the missionary apostle Paul. For Paul, 'a lateborn apostle', was an instrument chosen by God to preach the gospel (Gal 1.16; Acts 9.15). He was, in the concise phrase of C.K. Barrett, 'called by Christ to preach the gospel'. The gospel he preached was the same as that of Peter and the twelve: the risen Christ. Like all the apostles Paul received, believed, and preached the good news.

For I delivered to you as of first importance what I also received, that Christ died for our sins in accordance with the scriptures, that he was buried, that he was raised on the third day in accordance with the scriptures... Last of all, as to one untimely born, he appeared also to me (1 Cor 15.3-4,8).

For Paul preaching was of incomparable importance because faith in Christ the one mediator comes through hearing. He clearly stated more than once that preaching was the essential function of both himself and his collaborators. Preaching, for Paul, was a priestly work, 'to be a minister of Christ Jesus to the gentiles in the priestly service of the gospel of God' (Rom 15.6; cf. Phil 2.17).

The priestly service of preaching demands a lifetime of

15

preparation and dedication. Nevertheless the efficacy of Christian preaching is not contingent on the talent or skill of the preacher. Through hearing the gospel men are moved by the power of God to penitence and faith.

> My speech and my message were not in plausible words of wisdom, but in demonstration of the Spirit and power, that your faith might not rest in the wisdom of men but in the power of God (1 Cor 2.4-5).

Paul's preaching was primarily proclamation and teaching (2 Cor 15.18) but it was also his living example. 'I have been crucified with Christ; it is no longer I who live, but Christ who lives in me, and the life I now live in the flesh I live by faith in the Son of God' (Gal 2.20). Here perhaps Paul compares his preaching to that of Ezekiel who consumed God's word and thereby was assimilated to the Lord (Ezek 3.1f.). As a herald of the gospel Paul's preaching was bold and public but his person was subordinated to the very gospel he announced. The message, not the preacher, was all-important (Tit 1.3). He was a dedicated steward of the mysteries of God (1 Cor 4.1).

While presidency at the Eucharist is *the* great proclamation there is no explicit evidence in his letters that Paul regularly performed this service. By 'the cup which we bless' Paul almost certainly included himself (1 Cor 10.16), but the demands of his non-liturgical preaching surpassed cultic functions. This may be because Paul was engaged in proclaiming the gospel as a missionary. But it is also significant that Paul himself rarely baptized. Although he never forgot which communities he had founded through his preaching Paul had difficulty remembering those whom he had baptized!

> I am thankful that I baptized none of you except Chrispus and Gaias; lest any one should say that you were baptized in my name. (I did baptize also the household of Stephanas. Beyond that, I do not know whether I baptized any one else.) For Christ did not send me to baptize but to preach the gospel (1 Cor 1.14-17).

Paul also *corrected* those who strayed from his gospel. Paul counselled his co-preachers to be gentle when reprimanding God's people (2 Tim 2.25), but when necessary he could be stern with those who departed from his teaching.

> O foolish Galatians! Who has bewitched you, before whose eyes Jesus Christ was publicly portrayed as

16

crucified? Let me ask you only this: Did you receive the Spirit by works of the law, or by hearing with faith? Are you so foolish? Having begun with the Spirit, are you now ending with the flesh (Gal. 3.1-3; cf. 4.19)?

Paul found preaching so consuming that he thought of part-time ministry as an exception and not the rule. The minister of the gospel – if he was a true *minister* of the gospel – deserved financial support from those he served. Clearly then for Paul the 'worker-priest' was not the ideal. On the other hand, because preaching was so demanding, celibacy was the *ideal* but *not* necessarily connected with the ministry.

I wish that all were as I myself am. But each has his own special gift from God, one of one kind and one of another... Do we not have the right to our food and drink? Do we not have the right to be accompanied by a wife as the other apostles and the brothers of the Lord and Cephas? Or is it only Barnabas and I who have no right to refrain from working for a living. Who serves as a soldier at his own expense? Who plants a flock without getting some of the milk (1 Cor 7.7; 9.4-7)?

For Paul preaching was a demanding, exhausting, draining service that involved physical and mental suffering. The devoted minister of the word is a servant, a slave, a fool for the gospel message. He is a slave of his people (2 Cor 4.5) – even if this means he must spend hours each day *apart* from his people to study theology. He is a servant of the Church (Col 1.25) and of the gospel (Eph 3.7), the servant of his Lord who is the content of his preaching (1 Tim 4.6; 2 Cor 11.23). If preaching is informed, undiluted, and uncompromising, the preacher will sometimes be called a fool. The gospel is a keen, two-edged sword that cuts its servant deeply. 'We are fools for Christ's sake, but you are wise in Christ. We are weak, but you are strong. You are held in honour, but we in disrepute' (1 Cor 4.10).

Prophets and Teachers

The preaching of early prophets and teachers is important for today's ministry, not because all bishops and priests are prophets or teachers but because some of the preaching function of the early prophets and teachers were eventually absorbed by the triadic ministry of bishops, priests and deacons. Equally important, today's bishops and priests who have the major responsibility for preaching will effectively serve God's people only if they discern and heed today's prophets and teachers.

Prophets are rare and gifted persons appointed by God and called by the Spirit (1 Cor 14.1, 13-40). Prophets preach to the world and to individual Christians the salvation in Christ Jesus and the contemporary will of God. The prophet admonishes, consoles, and because he receives a revelation, pierces the secrets of human hearts (1 Cor 14.25).

The authority of a true prophet comes from God; but since many claim to be prophets, the claimant, be his claims explicit or implicit, must be discerned. Prophetic preaching is genuine when the prophet's words and life witness to Jesus Christ. Christ speaks through the prophet when the prophet's preaching is consonant with the foundational preaching of the apostles (1 Cor 12.3; Rom 12.6). Clearly then not all who claim the authority to preach as prophets are authentic spokesmen.

Test the spirits to see whether they are of God; for many false prophets have gone out into the world. By this you know the Spirit of God: every spirit which confesses that Jesus Christ has come in the flesh is of God, and every spirit which does not confess Jesus is not of God (1 Jn 4.1-3).

The prophet speaks from a future perspective and at times foretells future events (Acts 11.28; 1 Thess 3.4). But he also speaks pointedly to the present age. The prophet tells men how to act *now* in the present (Acts 15.32). His words build up, encourage, console, and preach repentance (1 Cor 14.3, 12). Those who heed him are instructed and encouraged (1 Cor 14.31). The Christian prophet is calm and direct; his preaching is not characterized by visions, voices or speaking in tongues. His message is the word of God which he communicates clearly.

It is significant that in many early communities prophets presided at the liturgy, the summit of Christian preaching (*Didache*, 15). In fact we have more explicit evidence for the liturgical ministry of prophets than we do for the apostles. This role of the prophet, especially his ministry at the Eucharist, was in the second century appropriated by bishops,

18

presbyters, and deacons. It is a role that continues to be exercised by the triadic ministry today.

The preaching of teachers, unlike that of the prophets, was founded not on a special revelation but was subject to the tradition. The teacher's ministry of the word was not intuitive but systematic; his preaching looked to the past but reinterpreted the gospel for the age with which he was engaged. Teachers also interpreted the Old Testament in the light of Christ. In brief, the gospel preached by the apostles was normative for the teacher's ministry. The apostles and prophets preached Christ; so did the teachers – and therefore they too deserved financial assistance. 'Let him who is taught the word share all good things with him who teaches' (Gal 6.6).

Paul considered teachers important servants of the Church. Not all Christians enjoyed the gift of teaching – which involved disciplined study – and Paul named teachers immediately after apostles and prophets. 'And God has appointed in the Church first apostles, second prophets, third teachers... Are all teachers?' (1 Cor 12.28-29)

To each Christian was given a gift for the common good. To each his own but for service of everyone. Teaching, like the other gifts, was for building up the body of Christ. 'Having gifts that differ according to the grace given to us, let us use them: if prophecy, in proportion to our faith; if service, in our serving; he who teaches, in his teaching' (Rom 12.6-7). However, the gift of teaching in the apostolic Church, then as today, was sometimes enjoyed by a person with other gifts as well. Paul himself was apostle, prophet, teacher, miracle worker, speaker in tongues... 'For this I was appointed a preacher and apostle..., a teacher of the gentiles in faith and truth.' (1 Tim 2.7)

Teachers were disciplined ministers of the word who not only studied the tradition but prayed and fasted (Acts 13.2-3). And like the prophets, teachers presided at the liturgy. Because they were grounded in the tradition the presidency of teachers served to nourish and unify God's people. But teachers, like the theologians who succeeded them, were sometimes ignored.

> ... Be unfailing in patience and in teaching. For the time is coming when people will not endure sound teaching, but having itching ears they will accumulate for themselves teachers to suit their own likings, and will turn away from listening to the truth and wander

into myths. As for you, always be steady, endure suffering, do the work of a evangelist, fulfil your ministry (2 Tim 4.2-5).

The Delegates of Paul

Late in the first century two companions of Paul, Timothy and Titus, were acting as his surrogates at Ephesus and Crete. These delegates of the apostles, like Paul himself, were unique to the primitive Church. But their preaching function continues. It was passed on to the officers they appointed and was eventually absorbed by bishops and presbyters.

Preaching was the delegate's consuming role. 'Preach the word, be urgent in season and out of season, convince, rebuke, and exhort, be unfailing in patience and in teaching' (2 Tim 4.2; Tit 2.1,15).

The delegate, like today's preachers, was to *preserve* the truth committed to the Church by the apostles. 'Follow the pattern of the sound words which you have heard from me, in the faith and love which are in Christ Jesus; guard the truth that has been entrusted to you by the Holy Spirit who dwells within us' (2 Tim 1.13-14; 3.14-17; Tit 2.1). But the delegate was more than a defensive reciter of orthodox formulae. He passed on the gospel in word and deed, in charity and faith. His teaching was creative and imaginative, as he interpreted the gospel for the time and place in which he served. Timothy was a skilled and creative preacher. As J. N. D. Kelly notes 'Paul is not saying that Timothy should reproduce his teaching word for word, still less that he had in mind some fixed creedal formula which he wants him to repeat without deviation.' (*A Commentary on the Pastoral Epistles*, London 1963, p. 166).

As he was Paul's delegate, it is not surprising that Timothy also corrected his brethren – but he was gentle and kind. 'And the Lord's servant must not be quarrelsome but kindly to every one, an apt teacher, forbearing, correcting his opponents with gentleness' (2 Tim 2.24). Timothy, the 'apt teacher', assumed the preacher function of Paul, who was his model. 'Hold fast the form of sound words, which thou hast heard of me, in faith and love which is in Christ Jesus' (2 Tim 1.13).

Therefore Timothy's preaching included the spoken word

20

and the witness of a good life, 'in speech and conduct, in love, in faith, in purity' (1 Tim 4.12). The gentle Timothy, like Paul, the other apostles, the prophets and teachers, would endure suffering. His preaching would not always be heeded (2 Tim 4.3-5 quoted on pages 19-20).

The apostolic delegates read the scriptures during worship, a function Paul mentions along with preaching and teaching. For the preaching of the gospel is grounded in God's word as recorded in the Bible. 'Till I come, attend to the public reading of scripture, to preaching, to teaching' (1 Tim 4.13).

We may safely presume that, as delegates of the apostle Paul, the delegates presided at the Eucharist. Yet there is no explicit evidence of their presidency. The point we are making is that their spoken ministry of the word is stressed throughout; their liturgical role, except for imposition of hands on presbyters is not; and their eucharistic role is not mentioned at all.

The delegates, like Paul himself, were to commission others to succeed *them*. Their successors would be residential Christian elders similar to the leaders in Jewish communities. Important for our purposes is Paul's reason for commissioning the delegates to appoint other community leaders. 'What you have heard from me before many witnesses entrust to faithful men who will be able to teach others also' (2 Tim 2.2). The torch was to be passed. Other officers were to be ordained to preach the gospel. These officers, appointed in late New Testament times by Paul himself (Acts 14.13) or by his delegates (1 Tim 3.1), were the *episcopoi-presbyteroi* (guardian-presbyters) of early Christian writings.

The Guardian-Presbyters

The guardian-presbyters are the officers in the apostolic Church who most closely resemble today's priests. In very few years one of these officers became a 'first among equals' until, early in the second century, the mono-episcopate had developed. What interests us here is the preaching role of the presbyteral college when the delegates were still in charge and *before* the mono-episcopate developed. We observe that, whereas the missionary apostles were on the move and innovative and the delegates more or less outside the local community, the guardian-presbyters were conservative of the foundation laid by the apostles and, very important, were within the local Church and chosen by that local Church as its ministers. These men therefore, were forerunners of today's priests who, like today's priests, preached the gospel in their native region.

The presbyters were commissioned to preserve and transmit the good news of Jesus Christ. 'What you have heard from me before many witnesses entrust to faithful men who will be able to teach others also' (2 Tim 2.2). Yet this ministry was an exigent one that demanded more than repetition of the apostolic preaching. The presbyters reinterpreted the gospel for their communities. This is a mission of delicate importance and may have contributed to Paul's caution about ordaining presbyters. 'Do not be hasty in the laying on of hands ' (1 Tim 5.22).

The guardian-presbyters, as successors of Paul and the delegates, were to correct those who betrayed the gospel. 'He must hold firm to the sure word as taught, so that he may be able to give instruction in sound doctrine and also to confute those who contradict it' (Tit 1.9). Clearly therefore the presbyter's task – especially those who taught and preached – was demanding. He *labours* in preaching and teaching – and for this reason deserves support.

> Let the elders who rule well be considered worthy of double honour, especially those who labour in preaching and teaching; for the scripture says, 'You shall not muzzle an ox when it is treading out the grain', and 'The labourer deserves his wages' (1 Tim 5.17-18).

There is some question among exegetes as to whether *all* of the earliest presbyters preached and taught or whether only an inner group provided this spoken service of the word, and there is the further question of whether only those who preached should be called *episcopoi-presbyteroi*. In the opinion of this writer *episcopos* is a generic term applicable to presbyters. It may well be that only certain members of the presbyteral college preached and taught. But even these officers did not represent a mono-episcopate such as developed later.

The guardian-presbyters excelled in the ministry of preaching both in word and example. 'Now the *episcopos* must be above reproach, the husband of one wife, temperate, sensible, dignified, hospitable, an apt teacher, no drunkard, not violent but gentle, not quarrelsome, and no lover

22

of money' (I Tim 3.2-3). We observe in passing that although Paul expected these men to be supported he does not expect a Christian minister to be affluent.

In Jerusalem the presbyters were present at the Jerusalem Council (Acts 15.4); and according to Luke, Paul thereafter reported to them on his progress with the gentiles (Acts 21.18). It is not surprising then that scripture uses shepherd symbolism of the presbyters.

> Tend the flock of God that is your charge, not by constraint but willingly, not for shameful gain but eagerly, not as domineering over those in your charge but being examples to the flock. And when the chief Shepherd is manifested you will obtain the unfading crown of glory (2 Pet 5.2-4; Acts 20.28).

Shepherd imagery connotes more than leadership; it also points to ministry of the word. In the Old Testament the shepherd guided, whistled, and gathered (Ps 28). Zechariah predicted that the Messiah, as shepherd, would suffer for his flock (Zech 13.1-6). Shepherds were teachers of their flocks (4 Ezr 5.18). In the New Testament pastors were teachers (Eph 4.11) who were to fight against false teaching (Acts 20.29), to be an example to their flocks (1 Pet 5.12) and to gather the scattered into one fold.

Finally, according to late New Testament evidence the presbyteral preaching role included not only spoken ministry of the world and imposition of hands but other sacramental functions. In the letter of James we notice that presbyters in Christ's name anointed the sick with prayer, a great preaching. 'Is any among you sick? Let him call for the elders of the Church, and let them pray over him, anointing him with oil in the name of the Lord' (James 5.14).

Conclusion

We have viewed various servants of the gospel at the origins of the Church whose preaching of the word, as the community ordered and reordered its ministry, was to be assumed by the developing leadership of bishops, presbyters, and deacons. In the New Testament there was a pluralism of Church officers. At Corinth there was a loosely structured community guided by Paul in which each had his special gift for service of the community (1 Cor 12.8f.). At

Paul's Philippi there were leaders called by the apostle *episcopoi* and *diakonoi* (Phil 1.1). At Thessalonia there were leaders who were 'over you in the Lord' (1 Thess 5.12), and at Ephesus there were pastor-teachers (Eph 4.11). At Jerusalem there were Peter and the twelve, James, and presbyters (Acts 6.15).

According to the Pastoral Epistles 'Paul' soon appointed delegates who were in turn commissioned to appoint presbyters in the Churches (1 Tim 3.1). The later canonical writings (e.g. 3 Jn 9) and the earliest non-canonical writings (e.g. 1 Clement 40) indicate that charismatic ordering was indeed waning, that the apostles were pillars of the past, that guardian-presbyters and deacons were succeeding prophets and teachers, that the complex development of the triadic ministry was well under way. How these and subsequent developments affected presbyteral preaching is the subject of our next chapter.

CHAPTER II

THE RISE OF THE PRESBYTER PREACHERS

During the early second century Christian ministry took a variety of forms. Prophets, teachers, and 'apostles' continued to serve in official capacities until their functions were considerably absorbed by the triadic ministry. However, even today there is unresolved tension concerning the preaching role of prophets and theologians on one hand and that of the ordained ministry on the other.

When the triadic ministry of bishop, presbyters and deacons was fully developed, the presbyters, at least until the fourth century, played a relatively modest role. The bishop was the paramount preacher in a community. The presbyters were his council who governed the Church with him and who were on occasion delegated to preside at the Eucharist and to preach the spoken word.

Paradoxically therefore the period in which the presbyterate developed as an order distinct from that of bishops was the period in the ministerial biography when presbyters were least active as preachers. Nevertheless where there was a church there were presbyters. And unlike permanent deacons the presbyters were not only there, they were there to stay. The rise of presbyter preachers is instructive for an understanding of the later priesthood.

1 Clement

Late in the first century (c. 95) Clement, a prominent Roman presbyter, wrote to the volatile Church at Corinth 'in the person of the Roman Church'. Clement's letter, like other contemporary writings, demonstrates the fluidity of early Christian ordering. A clear distinction between *episcopoi* and presbyters had yet to develop. The 'presbyters' were guardian-presbyters. Even if one of them were especially prominent, he was not the monarchical bishop of the second century.

At Corinth a cabal of jealous Corinthians had deposed

25

their guardian-presbyters. Clement argues forcefully for *order* in the Church. He draws analogies with the order in creation (20), in the army (7), in the human body (37), and in Old Testament priesthood. (40) In the analogy with levitical priesthood Clement is not *directly* proposing a theory of ministry but calling for order and obedience to authority.

We learn little about the functions of the presbyterate from Clement's letter – but what we do learn is consistent with the future development of episcopal and presbyteral preaching. Clement argues, rather simplistically, that God sent Christ, Christ appointed apostles, and the apostles appointed their 'first converts' as guardian-presbyters and deacons and arranged for a succession in this order. The preaching role of the guardian-presbyters is important; for Clement stresses the proclamation of the apostles whom the presbyters succeed.

> They went forth in the assurance of the Spirit preaching the good news (*evangelizomenoi*) that the kingdom of God is coming. They preached (*Kerussontes*) from district to district, and from city to city, and they appointed their first converts, testing them by the Spirit, to be bishops (presbyters) and deacons of future believers (44).

Guardian-presbyters also presided at the eucharistic liturgy, which was itself *the* great preaching and goal of preaching; for it which announced 'the death of the Lord until he comes'. 'He commanded us to celebrate sacrifices and services, and that it should not be thoughtlessly or disorderly, but at fixed times and hours.' (40) Clement admonishes the Corinthians for deposing the presbyters who were appointed by the apostles or other 'eminent men' and who presided at the Christian sacrifice.

> We consider therefore that it is not just to remove from their ministry those who were appointed by them, or later on by other eminent men, with the consent of the whole Church, and have ministered to the flock of Christ without blame, humbly, peaceably, and disinterestedly, and for many years have received a universally favorable testimony. For our sin is not small if we eject from the episcopate those who have blamelessly and holily offered its sacrifices (44).

It seems clear from Clement that at the century's turn ordering was still in transition, that some Churches were developing a presbyteral order similar to that of the Pastorals, that the development was not always linear nor without disruption, and that informed preaching of the gospel in leadership, word, liturgy and life was the presbyter's service to the community.

The Didache

The *Didache,* possibly reflecting a stage previous to Clement's Rome and Corinth, was compiled in Syria near the turn of the century. The Didache reflects Jewish-Christianity and gives evidence of successive stages in the development of Christian ministry and, therefore, of preaching. There seems to have been a time when 'apostles', prophets, and teachers were the most important officers in some communities. Eventually these ministers became resident officers in communities where, before long and with some tension, they were supplanted by *episcopoi* and deacons.

That the Eucharist is preaching is implied when the Didachist recommends that the prophets (your 'high priests') be given freedom to celebrate as they will. 'But suffer the prophets to hold Eucharist as they will' (10).

Teachers too presided at the Eucharist. Moreover, homilies by teachers, such as the epistle of Barnabas (c. 117 A.D.), were preserved and read aloud to the community. Much of their teaching function at the liturgy soon funnelled into the ministry of bishop, presbyter, and deacon.

Whoever then comes and teaches you concerning these things aforesaid, receive him. But if the teacher himself be perverted and teach another doctrine to destroy these things, do not listen to him, but if his teaching be for the increase of righteousness and knowledge of the Lord, receive him as the Lord (11).

The *Didache* also testifies to a somewhat later stage in ordering in which *episcopoi* and deacons were supplanting prophets and teachers in the ministry (*leiturgia*). For the word *episcopoi* in the *Didache* represents a collegial body and not monarchical bishops.

Appoint therefore for yourselves *episcopoi* and deacons worthy of the Lord, meek men and not lovers of money, and truthful and approved, for they also minister to you the ministry of the prophets and teachers. Therefore do not despise them, for they are your honourable men together with the prophets and teachers (15).

We conclude from the *Didache* that in Jewish Christianity late in the first century the ministry was in transition with 'apostles', prophets, teachers, *episcopoi* and deacons serving as authoritative ministers of the word. But this fluid ordering gradually yielded to a presbyteral order with one of the presbyters assuming a supervisory role.

Ignatius of Antioch and Polycarp of Smyrna

In the brief letters of Ignatius we observe that, early in the second century (c. 107), the triadic ministry was developing in Syria and Asia Minor. Henceforth in Churches with a single bishop the presbyterate is a subordinate body that co-operates with the bishop. The primary preacher in the small local Church is the bishop. He it is who leads the community, who presides at the Eucharist, and who gives the sermons. However, as we shall see, the presbyters were his important colleagues. Occasionally they were delegated to preach and even to preside at the Eucharist. When the time came in the fourth century for them to govern urban and rural communities and to preside regularly at the Eucharist their preaching role at that stage of reordering was consistent with previous developments.

All of you are to follow the bishop as Jesus Christ follows the Father, and the presbytery as the apostles. Respect the deacons as the command of God. Apart from the bishop no one is to do anything pertaining to the Church. A valid eucharist is to be defined as one celebrated by the bishop or by a representative of his. (Robert M. Grant, *The Apostolic Fathers, A new Translation and Commentary,* Vol. IV, *Ignatius of Antioch,* London, 1966, p. 120; but cf. James Mc-Cue, Bishops, Presbyters, and Priests in Ignatius of Antioch', *Theological Studies,* Vol. XXVIII, 1968, pp. 828-834).

In a letter to Bishop Polycarp of Smyrna, Ignatius exhorts him to stand firm in his teaching. 'Do not let those who seem plausible but teach strange doctrines buffet you. Stand firm as a hammered anvil' (Poly 3.1). Polycarp is to 'flee from evil arts, or indeed from preaching sermons about them' (5.1).

In the Ignatian ideal of Church order the ministry and indeed the Church itself was centered in the bishop. Yet his presbyters concelebrated with him, assisted at the sacraments and were, as his council, leaders in the Church. At Smyrna they were Polycarp's colleagues in teaching and in judging those who departed from the way. In Syria and Asia Minor the role of presbyters was primarily preaching in the wide sense; and on occasion this included preaching the spoken word of the good news of Jesus Christ.

The Shepherd of Hermas and 2 Clement

Later in the second century (c. 110-140), the anonymous Shepherd of Hermas was compiled at Rome for the Roman communities. This work reflects Jewish-Christianity, but makes use of biblical and Hellenistic materials.

It is significant, especially because Hermas wrote after Ignatius, that the author refers to presbyters *in globo*. The presbyteral order seems to have continued at Rome well into the second century. We learn little about these elders except that they performed a ministry of charity.

> The old lady came to me and asked if I had already given the book to the elders... But in this city you shall read it aloud with the elders who stand at the head of the Church (Vs ii, 4,3).

Graydon Snyder argues that this passage indicates 'that the Churches of Rome were unified by a presbyteral system' (*The Apostolic Fathers*, A New Translation and Commentary, Vol. VI, *Hermas*, London 1968, pp. 16-17).

But at least in some Roman communities the ministry was, or recently had been, pluralist. Hermas also refers to prophets, teachers, apostles, and deacons.

> The stones that are square and white and fit their joints are the apostles and bishops and teachers and deacons, who have sincerely and reverently served the elect of God as bishops and teachers and deacons (*ibid.* pp. 39-40).

The prophets of Hermas like the prophets of the *Didache* preached during the liturgy.

> The man who has the divine Spirit comes into an assembly of righteous men who have faith in the divine Spirit, and a prayer is made to God by the assembly of those men, then the angel of the prophetic Spirit

29

which is assigned to him fills the man, and that man, having been filled by the Spirit, speaks to the group as the Lord wills (*Mand.* 11).

In another context Hermas writes of apostles and teachers as men of the past. Significantly, they had proclaimed the good news. 'The apostles and teachers, who proclaimed the name of the Son of God, preached also to those who had previously fallen asleep' (*Sim.* ix, 16,5). However, teachers were still active even at Rome. According to Ephiphanius teachers and presbyters expelled the heretic Marcion from the Eternal City (Epiphanius, *Haer.* 42,2,2).

A contemporary of Hermas who wrote '2 Clement' testifies to a similarly fuild ministry. This letter, apparently a sermon to be read at communal worship, came from the pen of a teacher of Gentile-Christian background. The author describes the apostles as men of the past known from their writings which were becoming comparable to the holy writings of the Old Testament. 'Moreover the books and the apostles declare that the Church belongs not to the present, but has existed from the beginning' (xiv, 2). Presbyters now preached in the assembly and were to be obeyed.

And let us not merely seem to believe and pay attention now, while we are being exhorted by the Elders, but also when we have gone home let us remember the commandments of the Lord... Woe unto us, that it was there, and we knew it not, and did not believe, and were not obedient to the Elders, when they told us of our salvation (xvii, 3-5).

Justin

From the writings of Ignatius, Hermas, and 2 Clement it would seem that a single bishop emerged more slowly at Rome than is sometimes conjectured. The Roman apologist, Justin, is also silent about a Roman bishop. But his silence, especially in an epoch of persecutions, should not be pressed. Eusebius narrates that the great traveller Hegesippus drew up a Roman succession 'up to Anicetus' (c. 155). Eusebius does not recount that sucession, but it seems that within Justin's lifetime (c. 110-165) the presbyterate took shape as a distinct body even at Rome (Eusebius, *Ecclesiastical History*, III, 37; cf. IV, 22). Presbyters participated in the bishop's ministry of the word.

Justin informs us of four details significant for the preaching ministry: the commuity was responsible for instruction of the catechumens, the president at the Eucharist was free to improvise, the people participated at least by saying 'Amen', and after baptism the new members joined in the prayers and Eucharist. All Christians therefore share apostolic succession in proclamation of the good news.

> Having concluded the prayers we greet one another with a kiss. Then there is brought to the president of the brethren bread and a cup of water and of watered wine; and taking them he gives praise and glory to the Father of all, through the name of the Son and of the Holy Spirit, and he himself gives thanks at some length in order that these things may be deemed worthy.
>
> When the prayers and thanksgiving are completed, all the people present call out their assent saying: 'Amen'... After the president has given thanks, and all the people have shouted their assent, those whom we call deacons give to each one present to partake of the Eucharistic bread and wine and water; and to those who are absent they carry away a portion (Justin Martyr, *First Apology* in W. A. Jurgens, *The Faith of the Early Fathers*, Collegeville 1970, p.55).

In another passage we notice again that the president is free to improvise at the liturgy, that he gives a homily, and that he 'takes care of all who are in need'. We know that in the early communities the bishop was responsible for those in need; therefore the president may have been a bishop or a presbyter delegated by him.

> When the reader has finished, the president verbally gives a warning and appeal for the imitation of these good examples. Then we all rise together and offer prayers, and, as we said before, when our prayer is ended, bread is brought forward along with wine and water, and the president likewise gives thanks to the best of his ability, and the people call out their assent, saying the *Amen* (*ibid*. p.56).

One final point about Justin is noteworthy – Justin himself. Justin was a teacher. Despite the gradual structuring of a priestly hierarchy – Tertullian was soon to describe the bishop as 'high priest' – teachers still served the communities. In Justin's time they assisted with the catechumens but apparently were not acknowledged as Church officers commissioned to preside or preach at the Eucharist.

Irenaeus was born in Asia Minor where as a youth he studied under Polycarp. Eventually he 'exchanged figs for frogs' becoming an important presbyter at Lyons in Gaul and, in 177, the second bishop of that Church. He was not to be the last of the Fathers to become a bishop-theologian. His great work *Adversus Haereses* was written during his years as bishop.

The apostles and their successors commited the Churches to 'bishops' who because of their *charism of truth* assured succession in apostolic teaching. Irenaeus emphasized the lists of bishops who traced their genealogy to an apostle or successor of an apostle. What was at stake was no tactile theory of orders but succession in apostolic truth, a succession in traditional teaching assured by Churches whose bishops descended from an apostle.

> It is possible, then, for everyone in every Church, who may wish to know the truth, to contemplate the tradition of the apostles which has been made known throughout the whole world. And we are in a position to enumerate those who were instituted bishops by the apostles, and their successors to our own times, men who neither knew nor taught anything like these heretics rave about (iii,3,1).

On occasion Irenaeus calls the bishops 'presbyters'.

> It is necessary to obey those who are presbyters in the Church, those who, as we have shown, have succession from the apostles, those who have received, with the succession of the episcopate, the sure charism of truth according to the good pleasure of the Father (iv, 26,2).

He is not speaking here of a presbyteral college but of the bishops themselves, probably comparing them to the ancients who knew the apostles. In other writings such as the *Presentation of the Apostolic Preaching,* and in a fragment, by 'presbyters' Irenaeus means great men of antiquity.

Tertullian, the first great Latin writer, was a North African lawyer and convert. Like many subsequent converts Tertullian was a rigorist. Eventually he was attracted by the rigorist Montanist heresy, but his earlier writings (c. 197-206) reflect the Catholic scene. According to Tertullian the apostolic rule of faith, as opposed to esoteric gnostic traditions, was safeguarded by Churches founded by an apostle or an associate of an apostle and by Churches in communion with those apostolic Churches. Taking liberties with the complex history of the ministry Tertullian argued that the apostles appointed monarchical bishops to succeed them. Like Irenaeus he resorted to lists of bishops tracing their origins to an apostle as a sure sign of succession in apostolic doctrine.

Tertullian's theory on the ministry was never worked out. But from his great apology we learn that presbyters read scriptures in public, gave sermons, corrected the brethren, and passed judgment.

> We assemble to recall the divine scriptures... In the same place there are exhortations, corrections and divine censure. Judgment is passed with the greatest of gravity, as among men who are certain of the presence of God; and it is the greatest foretaste of the future judgement, when anyone has sinned so grievously that he is cut off from communication in prayer and assembly and from every holy transaction. Certain approved elders preside, who have received that honour not for a price but by the witness of character (Tertullian, *Apology*, in Jurgens, *Faith of the Early Fathers*, p. 115).

In a treatise *on Baptism* we come upon the developed structure of bishop, presbyters, deacons, and laity. Already in Tertullian's time the 'clergy' was being elevated above the laity. Tertullian calls the bishop 'high priest' and so implies the priesthood of presbyters. Later, as a Montanist, he will refer more clearly to the priesthood of presbyters. The clergy is an *ordo*. In Tertullian's words about the ministers of baptism we see the close association of presbyters with the bishop who, in his absence, had the primary right to baptize.

> In giving it [baptism], certainly, the primary right is had by the high priest, that is, the bishop, and after him, the presbyters and the deacons, though not without authority from the bishop, on account of the honour of the Church, for, when this is preserved, peace is preserved. Besides these even a layman has the right (*Tertullian's Homily on Baptism*, Ernest Evans, ed., London 1964, pp. 5-36).

In North Africa therefore presbyters were approved men of character closely associated with the bishop who was the

Christian high priest. They shared in his preaching ministry, which meant that on occasion they presided at the liturgy and preached in the strict sense.

The Apostolic Tradition

The Apostolic Tradition of Hippolytus is an important third-century Church order which, especially in its ordination rite for presbyters, reflects the role of presbyters in the second and third centuries. This conservative order of rite and polity was compiled early in the third century by the Roman presbyter, theologian, rigorist, sometimes anti-Pope, and martyr, Hippolytus of Rome. Hippolytus, a student of Irenaeus and Tertullian, was ordained a presbyter by Pope Victor in 190.

Hippolytus' career as a presbyter is itself an indication that on occasion presbyters preached in the strict sense. When the renowned Alexandrian teacher, Origen, visited Rome it is reported by Eusebius that Hippolytus, while still a presbyter in communion with the Pope, preached in Origen's presence. From the slim evidence we possess it seems that presbyters occasionally were acknowledged as homilists but that teachers were not. Teachers at Alexandria and at Rome were under official control. In neither Church were they ordained.

After the death of Pope Zephyrinus the presbyter Hippolytus drifted into schism. Until his reconciliation some years later as a martyr he was leader of a small sect which repudiated the alleged laxism and modalism of Pope Callistus. Hippolytus objected to the ordination of remarried men and to the marriage of ministers.

Before lapsing into schism Hippolytus compiled the *Apostolic Tradition* to bolster traditional rite and practice. This conservative document reflects the practice of Rome, and to a lesser extent, Syria and Asia Minor. The *Tradition* and other Church orders were widely circulated in Syria and Egypt from the third to fifth centuries.

However, even today the *Apostolic Tradition* has left a visible imprint on the Churches of Ethiopia, in the Roman liturgy, and in monophysite communities. It continues to reflect and influence belief and practice. When a contemporary Catholic community celebrates Mass according to the second canon of the Roman missal they are indebted to

Hippolytus and to the Roman communities who worshipped before and after he compiled the *Apostolic Tradition*.

Our concern with the *Apostolic Tradition* focuses on the ordination-rite for presbyters, which in turn is elucidated by other passages in the document. We shall see that presbyters were intimately and inseparably conjoined to the bishop in his pastorate.

The bishop-elect was chosen by the people. Thereafter on a Sunday, 'the Lord's day', this election was ratified by the people, presbyters and other bishops who were present. The bishops, laying hands on the nominee, consecrated him 'and the presbyters stand by in silence'. In the consecration-prayer it is announced that the bishop succeeds to the role of Christ and the apostles. He is prince, pastor and high priest. The Church therefore was explicitly acknowledging the priesthood of bishops, an acknowledgement that was adumbrated as early as the time of Clement of Rome and stated forcefully by Tertullian. The bishop was high priest because he presided at the Christian sacrifice, forgave sins, and was empowered to bind and loose. His central place in the community is reflected in the prayer for his grace of office.

> And now pour forth that Power which is from thee, of 'the princely Spirit' which thou didst deliver to thy Beloved Servant Jesus Christ, which he bestowed on thy holy apostles who established the Church... Father who knowest the hearts of all, grant upon this thy servant whom thou hast chosen for the episcopate to feed thy flock and serve as thine high priest, that he may minister blamelessly by night and day, that he may unceasingly behold and propitiate thy countenance and offer to thee the gifts of the holy Church, and that by the high priestly Spirit he may have authority 'to forgive sins' according to thy bidding, to 'loose every bond' according to the authority thou gavest to the apostles, and that he may please thee in meekness and a pure heart, 'offering' to thee 'a sweet-smelling savour' (Gregory Dix, *The Treatise on the Apostolic Tradition of Saint Hippolytus,* London, 1968, pp. 4-6).

The presbyters share the bishops' priesthood in a surbordinate way. They alone, and not the deacons, lay hands on the oblation during the concelebrated Eucharist that follows episcopal consecration.

In the ordination-rite for a presbyter the other presbyters join the bishop in laying hands on the ordinand. This is because they share in the spirit common to the presbyterate; but presbyters do *not* ordain. 'For the presbyter has authority only for this one thing, to receive. But he has no authority to give holy orders.' Presbyters do not impose hands on a deacon because a deacon does not share in the priesthood. 'He is not ordained for a priesthood, but for the service of the bishop...' Without explicitly calling the presbyters 'priests' the rite clearly reflects their priesthood.

The prayer at the ordination of a presbyter asks that he may receive the spirit of grace and counsel, that he may share in the presbyterate, and that he may help and govern God's people. The spirit of grace is the grace of ministry imparted by the Spirit. The spirit of counsel (*pneuma sumboulias*) is the grace to serve as the bishop's council and, therefore, to rule God's people. The 'help and govern' recall the gifts of leadership included by Paul in the charismata of early Corinth. The collective leadership of the presbyters as the bishop's council is further symbolized by the analogy with the elders who governed with Moses.

O God and Father of our Lord Jesus Christ – Look upon this thy servant and impart to him the spirit of grace and counsel, 'that he may share' in the presbyterate and help and govern thy people with a pure heart.

As thou didst look upon the people of thy choice and didst command Moses to choose presbyters whom thou didst fill with the Spirit which thou hadst granted to thy minister.

So now, O Lord, grant that there may be present among us unceasingly the Spirit of thy grace, and make us worthy that in faith we may minister to thee in singleness of heart praising thee (*ibid.* pp. 15-16).

The presbyter's ministry of the word may be illustrated in the rite for baptism. The presbyter accepts on behalf of the Church the catechumen's renunciation of Satan, he exorcises, anoints, and officiates at the profession of faith. As the ceremony concludes the presbyter baptizes the new member. Here in word, deed and symbol the presbyter's leadership 'is exercised primarily though the word' (Küng).

Nevertheless, the pre-eminent preacher in both the wide and strict sense was the bishop. The presbyters as his council participated in his preaching. We know from the pulpit-

36

preaching of the presbyter Hippolytus that presbyters on occasion gave homilies in Church. But in the third century this was not the common practice. Presbyters were less active and indeed less necessary as ministers of the word than they would be in the future.

The Didascalia

Another third-century Church order, *The Didascalia*, likewise exalts the bishops, but, unlike the *Apostolic Tradition*, the Didascalia is very favourable to deacons. The anonymous author according to the literary convention of his day claims apostolic authorship. In fact the compiler was probably a bishop in Syria. He was also a merciful man, less concerned with legislation than with pastoral and ethical affairs and the reconciliation of repentant sinners.

In the *Didascalia* the bishop, compared to God the Father, is the centre of unity in the Church. He is mediator, high priest and king who, assisted by his deacons, provided for the poor. He in turn is provided for by his people.

> You then today, O bishops, are priests to your people, and the Levites who minister to the tabernacle of God, the holy Catholic Church, who stand continually before the Lord God. You then are to your people priests and prophets, and princes and leaders and kings, and mediators between God and his faithful, and receivers of the word and preachers and proclaimers thereof, and knowers of the scriptures and of the utterances of God and witnesses of his will who bear the sins of all and are to give an answer for all (R. H. Connolly, *Didascalia Apostolorum*, Oxford 1929, p.80).

The author frequently refers to the bishop's ministry of the word. As pastor the bishop preaches in the rooms where the community gathers for worship, teaches his flock, and explains the sayings of scripture. 'Be diligent therefore and attentive to the word, O bishop, so that, if thou canst, thou explain every saying: that with much doctrine thou mayst abundantly nourish and give drink to thy people.'

The presbyters, as the bishop's council, help him to govern the people. Their place at the Eucharist reflects their role in the community. They sit with the bishop at the east end of the church, and probably concelebrate with him. 'And for

37

the presbyters let them be assigned a place in the eastern part of the house, and let the bishop's throne be set in their midst, and let the presbyters sit with him.'

As at the Rome of Hippolytus, presbyters baptized; but so did the deacons. Presbyters, with the bishop, passed judgement; but so did the deacons. Significantly, however, the deacons were compared to Christ in his servant role, the presbyters to the apostles.

In the two Church orders we have described the Church is centred in the bishop. But as the bishop's council, as concelebrants around his chair, as judges of the community and on occasion leaders at liturgy, presbyters were important ministers of the word. Their preaching in the strict sense was in part circumscribed by the small size of the room where the Christians gathered.

Origen

The developing role of presbyters is further portrayed in the varied career and writings of Origen. As an authorized but not ordained teacher, Origen was a layman. Origen himself soon realized the need for scientific study of scripture and philosophy. Therefore he delegated the task of rudimentary instruction to his former pupil, Heraclas, and concentrated on research and instruction of the advanced.

In 216 Origen paid a fateful visit to Caesarea in Palestine. There, as a lay theologian, he explained scripture in the assembly. When his own bishop, Demetrius of Alexandria, learned of this he was furious. The bishops of Palestine defended Origen and argued that charismatic teachers sometimes preached. Teachers were not among the clergy but *assisted* the clergy.

> In cases where persons are found duly qualified to assist the clergy, they are called on by the holy bishops to preach to the laity; e.g. in Laranda, Euelpius; in Iconium, Paulinus; in Synnada, Theodore were called on respectively by Neon, Celsus, and Atticus, our blessed brother-bishops. Probably there are other places too where this happens, unknown to us (Eusebius, *Ecclesiastical History*, 6,19,lf).

Origen returned to Alexandria where as a lay *didaskalos,* he pressed on with his research, writing and teaching. In 222 he was summoned to Greece to assist the Churches there in the struggle against heresy. He paid a second fateful visit to Caesarea and, without his bishop's permission, was ordained a presbyter. This irregular ordination is significant because it seems Origen accepted ordination as a presbyter *so that he could preach in the strict sense*. As we have already observed, presbyters were beginning to preach, at least on occasion; and as we have seen in Origen's own experience the teaching charism was becoming absorbed by the triadic ministry who were the 'official teachers'. Lay *didaskaloi* would continue to function but they were under the control of the ordained leadership. Bishop, presbyters, and deacons were the ordinary preachers in Christian assemblies.

When the Church at Alexandria censured him for his irregular ordination Origen moved to Caesarea. Preaching, including preaching to the bishop, was a preoccupation of his life. The harmony that prevailed between Origen, the priest-theologian of Caesarea, and the Palestinian bishops is an example of co-operation between bishop and theologian. The earlier friction between Origen, the lay theologian of Alexandria, and the Egyptian bishops is an example of the unseemly disharmony between bishop and theologian that was to erupt periodically throughout Christian history.

Origen preached almost every day in his later years – and from 246 his homilies were recorded by scribes. He was more concerned with the sacrament of the spoken word than with the liturgy. He argued that when the faithful hear the word of God they are enabled to worship daily in spirit and in truth. For Origen the priest's sacrifice and immolation was preaching the word of God.

Altars are no longer moist with the blood of beasts; they are hallowed by Christ's precious blood. Priests and levites do not now administer the blood of goats and bulls, by the grace of the Holy Spirit they dispense the word of God (*Hom. Lev.* 10.1).

In his homily on Joshua Origen writes in the same vein: 'When you see priests and levites no longer handling the blood of rams and bulls, but ministering the word of God by the grace of the Holy Spirit, then you can say that Jesus has taken the place of Moses' (*Hom. Josh* 2,6).

For Origen, preaching in the strict sense was informed proclamation *and explanation of* the word. The preacher had to be conversant with theology, a man of prayer, and, in brief, an inspired servant of the word who understood, proclaimed, and faithfully explained scripture. 'What good

39

is it to me to be enthroned at the master's desk in the place of honour... if I cannot do the work my position demands' *(Hom. Ezech. 5,4)*.

In Origen's reply to Celsus we learn that Christian preaching in the third century was proclamation of the central truths of Christians; it was preaching of Jesus Christ. But these central truths cannot be merely announced; they must be explained to God's people.

> Since he frequently calls the Christian doctrine a secret system, we must confute him on this point, also since almost the entire world is better acquainted with what Christians preach than with the favourite opinions of philosophers. For who is ignorant of the statement that Jesus was born of a virgin, and that he was crucified and that his resurrection is an article of faith among many, that a general judgment is announced to come in which the wicked are to be punished according to their deserts, and the righteous to be duly awarded? *(Contra Celsum 1,7)*.

Origen's writings provide insights for understanding the role of Christian priesthood, Christian preaching, and the connection between the two. Origen's own life suggests that Church leaders and theologians should learn from one another and co-operate in building up the Church. When the charisms of leadership and of theology are divorced from one another the Church suffers. Origen suggests that the priest must be 1) a man of prayer and 2) a disciplined student of scripture and theology. His primary role is not liturgy (preaching in the wide sense) but ministry of the word. As Cardinal Jean Daniélou notes, 'as a *didaskalos* he stressed the sacrament of preaching much more than the sacrament of the liturgy... He was interested in the visible signs of worship only in so far as they were signs of spiritual things.' *(Origen,* N.Y. 1955, p.42).

In his fervent insistence on the primacy of preaching Origen was not always heeded by subsequent priests. This was almost certainly an impoverishment. But Origen is a man for all seasons. His career as a teacher and later as a priest-teacher is instructive for questions being asked today.

When we turn to Origen's contemporary, Cyprian of Carthage, we meet a churchman whose life differed antithetically from Origen's in many ways. Unlike Origen, Cyprian was for a good part of his life a pagan orator. In 246 he was converted and shortly thereafter, while still a neophyte, consecrated bishop of Carthage. Cyprian's conversion took place too late in life for him to become a refined theologian and exegete. Moreover, his episcopate was beset by turmoil, controversy, persecution, exile, and martyrdom. Cyprian relied on scripture and the writings of Tertullian, both of which he interpreted quite literally. His theological presuppositions and his exegesis of some texts of scripture have pervasively influenced the Church.

Cyprian founded the Church's unity on the episcopate. He applied Old Testament texts on Jewish priesthood quite literally to Christian ministry. Cyprian therefore has been largely responsible for the comparison of Christian ministry to Jewish priesthood. How authentic this development, begun as early as I Clement, is, remains a matter of controversy.

According to Cyprian's exegesis of the New Testament Christ appointed followers as apostles or 'bishops and overseers'. These in turn stood in the place of God and appointed successors (Ep. 54.3). Presbyters presided over every Church in communion with the bishop. In his absence they guided the Church. When Cyprian was in exile during the Decian persecution he wrote to his presbyters and deacons:

... as the condition of the place does not permit me to be with you now, I beg you, by your faith and your religion, to discharge there both your own offices and mine, that there may be nothing wanting either to discipline or diligence (Ep. 4.1).

Cyprian adapted Church practice to meet the unprecedented challenges of his own episcopate. He was not constrained by the practice of bygone decades nor by the practice in other Churches during his own lifetime. During his episcopate presbyters were on occasion delegated to preside at the sacraments. This does not mean they were presidents of urban or rural communities. But the scope of responsibility delegated to them would have included the giving of homilies. '... Presbyters also who there offer the oblation with the confessors may severally take their turns with a different deacon' (Ep. 5.1).

Significantly, presbyters instructed catechumens and examined the readers, 'examining whether in both all things corresponded to what ought to be found in such as are being prepared for the clergy' (Ep. 29). Cyprian, like Origen, is insisting that candidates for the clergy should be well-informed in the word of God and exemplary in holiness of life.

Conclusion

Preaching in the wide sense is witnessing to the gospel in leadership, word, liturgy and life. In the second and third centuries the foremost preacher in this wide sense was the bishop. Preaching in the strict sense is the spoken proclamation of the word, especially through the homily at the Eucharist, when the Christian community gathers to worship. Here too the leader in this ministry was the bishop. But in the third century, as the Church grew in numbers, the bishops became increasingly dependent on presbyters. These were his inseparable co-priests, co-leaders, co-preachers who were on occasion delegated to preach the homily at worship.

CHAPTER III

THE PRIEST AS PREACHER IN THE MIDDLE AGES

As the Church expanded, one Eucharist, in one consecrated room, presided over by the bishop and his presbyterium was no longer feasible in any populated region. The pagan historian Porphyry and the Christian historian Eusebius both testify that at the turn of the fourth century Christians were building churches (Jean Daniélou & Henri Marrou, *The Christian Centuries*, N.Y. 1964, p. 224).

The presbyters, who had served as the bishop's council and who on occasion presided at the Eucharist, were the logical persons to be called upon to meet the unprecedented challenge. An early council at Vaison reflects the situation after Constantine, wherein presbyters celebrated the Eucharist for local communities, anointed the sick, administered baptism, led penitents to reconciliation and preached the word of God in Church. In the remainder of this study our primary concern will be this foremost role of 'priest of the second rank': preaching the gospel to God's gathered people.

At Rome the presbyters were delegated by the bishop to preach in titular and cemetery churches but only gradually did they take charge of communities. In Gaul and Spain the churches were less centralized and presbyters soon fanned out to serve rural communities in the villages and demesnes.

Pope Leo the Great (c. 450) argued that bishops should be consecrated rather sparingly and that priests should preside in 'less important' municipalities. In general the policy for which Leo contended, was, with notable exceptions, the one that prevailed.

> Where the people are less important and the assemblies less numerous, it is sufficient that they be confided to the care of presbyters. Bishops should govern only over greater people and larger cities, so that the divinely inspired decrees of the holy Fathers may be observed, which forbid the priestly dignity of bishop to be given to hamlets or demesnes, or to obscure and isolated municipalities, lest that office, to which only

the more important duties should be confided, become cheap by very reason of the great number who hold it (*Epist.* XII, X PL 54,654).

In this chapter we shall focus mainly but not exclusively on some important ordination rites which reflect the Church's belief and practice in the centuries from Constantine. Because the liturgy, while it is an indispensable source for the belief, teaching, and practice of the Church, does not always perfectly reflect that practice, we shall at the conclusion of this chapter take note of the rise and decline of friar preachers at the close of the middle ages.

Before turning to the ordination rites we should recall two concurrent trends, one theological and one practical, which coexisted with the ordination of presbyters to preside over and preach to local communities.

First there was, among many theologians, the theory known as parity of ministers. The first to expound this theory was an anonymous Roman priest of the fourth century, Ambrosiaster, who was concerned about the power of the Roman deacons. He was followed by the influential Jerome. Under the names of these two men (Ambrosiaster was for centuries thought to be Ambrose or Augustine) this theory was transmitted to the middle ages. Basically the theory of parity maintains that originally *episcopoi* and *presbyteroi* were the same persons. The subsequent distinction between bishop and priests was a matter of the authority given to the bishop, which authority, including the power to confirm and consecrate, was given to him by ecclesiastical custom. As far as priesthood is concerned bishop and presbyter are equal, a 'parity' of ministers. At the twilight of the western patristic age Isidore of Seville, as was then the custom, compiled some passages from Jerome. Many writers, not adverting to the whole context of Isidore's writings on the ministry, have since included him among the proponents of parity. In fact, however, Isidore seems closer to the doctrine contained in the early ordination rites and reiterated at Vatican II. Nevertheless, the theory of parity was repeated by many compilers and endorsed by several of the great scholastics.

The second trend under way was the practice of absolute ordination, or the ordination of presbyters not for the service of a diocesan bishop. The situation conducive to this practice appears in a life of Ceolfrith, a monk at Jarrow. Benedict Biscop, founder of Jarrow and Monkwearmouth,

44

is alleged to have sought out Ceolfrith 'who might both strengthen the observance of the regular life by a zeal for learning equal to his own, and also, being in priest's orders, discharge the service at the altar.' (Bede, *A History of the English Church & People*, L. Sherly-Price, ed., Baltimore, 1968, p. 26). Moreover, some priests were ordained to say Mass in the chapels of wealthy lords and ladies. The relation of the ministry of these men to their bishop was ambivalent at best. Their preaching was in many cases either non-existent or deficient even for an unlettered age. Finally there was the consecration of *chorepiscopoi*, monkbishops who ordained monks and performed some episcopal services for the laity but where by no means the residential bishop surrounded by a presbyterium as we have seen the latter structures develop in the early Church. Absolute ordination was an abuse and its effects still smoulder in the ordination of monks and regulars who rarely, if ever, preach to God's people.

The Testament of Our Lord

In Syria early in the fifth century there was compiled an apocrhyphal Church order, similar to *The Apostolic Tradition*, called *The Testament of Our Lord*. Like the *Apostolic Tradition* this order included an ordination rite and prescriptions for ministers. This document reflects the eastern scene when Churches were proliferating despite heresies and sporadic persecution and when presbyteral preaching was on the increase. The rite was influential in Syria, Asia Minor, Abyssinia, Egypt, and among some monophysite Churches. Even today traces of it may be discerned in some Ethiopic liturgies.

In the *Testament of Our Lord*, as in the later western liturgies, the sanctity of the priest was of paramount importance. He was, moreover, to read and preach the gospel to God's people, 'skilled in reading, meek, poor, not moneyloving, having laboured much in ministrations among the weak, proud to be pure, without blame' (29).

At ordination the bishop and presbyters laid hands upon the ordinand, the bishop praying for the Spirit of grace and of reason and of strength, the Spirit of the presbyterate. Presbyters are compared to the Jewish elders who were filled with the Spirit by God and who assisted Moses to govern the people of the Covenant. Their preaching role is reflected when they are compared to the disciples chosen by Christ.

After the analogy with the elders and disciples the prayer goes on to petition that the presbyter be a worthy pastor who will feed God's people.

And make him worthy of being filled with thy wisdom and thy hidden mysteries to feed thy people in holiness of heart; pure, and true; praising, blessing, lauding, giving thanks, offering a doxology always day and night, to thy holy and glorious Name...

The presbyter is not expected to preach recondite theology but such things 'that the people may remember.' At the Last Judgement he will give an account for his preaching – indeed he will repeat what he taught his people and they in turn will be punished if they did not heed his words. In addition to preaching in Church, presbyters, accompanied by a deacon, visited and instructed the sick.

Let the presbyter, as is right and fitting, go about to the houses of those who are sick with the deacon, and visit them, let him consider and say to them those things that are fitting and proper, especially to the faithful (31).

Teaching, therefore, in addition to proclamation was an important function of the presbyterate as we see it reflected in *The Testament of Our Lord*. It was the duty of presbyters to strengthen 'those who have newly become catechumens with prophetical and evangelical utterances, with the word of teaching' (31).

The Statuta Ecclesiae Antiqua

In these same centuries there were circulating in the west collections of rubrical directives and legislation. The *Statuta Ecclesiae Antiqua* was compiled in Gaul during the fifth century. This document gives some indication of the developing rites for consecration and ordination in Gaul. The author is vigorously pro-presbyteral and anxious to restrict the powers being preempted by deacons. The bishop, with his presbyterate scattered, could and at times did become autocratic. Moreover, with presbyters presiding over local communities deacons could and at times did appear to be assuming roles proper to the presbyterate. For these reasons

46

the compiler of the *Statuta* insists that presbyters should have a say in the appointment of ordinands, that they are superior to deacons, that the bishop should seek their counsel in passing judgement, and that they should retain responsibility for Church property.

The author of the *Statuta* is concerned that local presidents should share collegially in the bishop's government of the whole Church. Important for our purposes is that the development of local presidents meant that priests were the central preachers in the strict sense in those communities. One of the purposes of the bishop's retention of the right to ordain and of his prerogative of visitation was to assure the reliability of the presbyters' proclamation and teaching in church.

The bishop remained the foremost preacher in the wider community. Nevertheless, presbyters, as his council and, more important still, as leaders in their own right, were, because of the expansion of the Church, the most important preachers in Christendom. The Church had restructed itself in such a way that the priest had responsibility for nourishing the gathered community with the word. Upon the preaching of parish or secular priests, for weal or woe, hinged the self-understanding, growth, and reconciling mission of the people of God.

The Verona Ordination-Rite

In fifth or sixth century Rome there was compiled a detailed sacramentary, including an ordination-rite for a presbyter, sometimes called the Leonine sacramentary. The earliest version to come down to us is a seventh-century copy now preserved at Verona – hence the alternate name for the book, the Sacramentary of Verona.

The Verona ordination rite is in the tradition of the rite of Hippolytus and the Church orders. But it is an original composition by an author familiar with the Roman Church. Before long, as we shall see, the Roman rite was conflated with rites in use in Gaul from the sixth to eighth centuries. By comparing the Verona version with these later conflations we can reasonably reconstruct the original Roman rite.

In the early Roman rite there were three ordination prayers: a bidding, a collect, and a prayer of consecration. From these prayers, especially the prayer of consecration, we can perceive something of the functions of presbyters in the early middle ages.

The Verona rite and other contemporary Christian writings took over for Christian usage many of the terms used for dignitaries in the Roman state. These terms were adapted and applied to Christian ministry. This clearly reflects another development under way, especially at Rome, at the time. The ministry, especially the triadic 'hierarchy', was being elevated above the *plebs* or laity; ministers of the Church were conceived of as belonging to an 'order' or 'grade' above those not ordained. Equally significant is the fact that while the rites presumed the priesthood of presbyters, these were called priests 'of the second rank' or 'co-operators of our [the episcopal] order.' The bishop was the one high priest in his Church. But priests of the second rank were, in their turn, a grade or order higher than deacons who were told to aspire to the higher grades.

In the three prayers of the Verona ordination-rite there is throughout a pervasive emphasis on priestly holiness. The ordinand is transfigured and changed by ordination. His priestly conduct and example – a form of preaching in the wide sense – is an important aspect of his ministry.

The Christian priesthood is portrayed as the fulfilment of levitical priesthood which both foreshadowed and prepared for it. The bishop is high priest, successor to Aaron; he is also successor to Moses and, where preaching is concerned, successor to the apostles. The priests of the second rank are successors to the sons of Aaron; they are also successors to the seventy elders who governed with Moses and, where preaching is concerned, successors to the disciples who assisted the apostles.

In the bidding-prayer the people are requested to invoke the heavenly gifts of God the Father upon the man he has chosen for the office (*munus*) of presbyter.

> Let us pray, dearly beloved, to God the Father Almighty that, upon these his servants, whom he has chosen for the office of presbyter, he may multiply heavenly gifts, with which what they have begun by his favour they may accomplish by his aid (*The Ordination Prayers of the Ancient Western Churches*, H. B. Porter, ed., London 1967, p. 25).

The collect which follows presents to God the men he has chosen. The people ratify God's choice and petition for the minister the gift of his Spirit and grace.

Hear us, O God of our salvation, and pour forth the benediction of the Holy Spirit and the power of priestly grace upon these thy servants, that thou mayest accompany with the unfailing riches of thy bounty those whom we set before thy merciful countenance to be consecrated (*ibid.*).

Three points about the prayer of consecration are especially significant. First, the prayer employs terms signifying special rank, such as *dignitas, honor, ordo,* and *gradus.* Dignity connoted the inherent worthiness of the office and its occupant, honour distinguished him from other persons, order was a collective term which designated a group distinguished from other (in this case, lower) orders or from the people in general, grade signified the particular order occupied in the ascending grades or *cursus honorum.* These contemporary terms are baptized with a new and Christian meaning. They now connote roles involving service to God and men. Secondly, the consecration prayer refers to Christian ministry as an unfolding of divine providence. All things have been divinely arranged in due order – including levitical priesthood and the Christian ministry which fulfils it. In attributing divine providence to the unfolding of Jewish and Christian priesthood the prayer compares the bishop to the Jewish high priest (*summus pontifex*) and the presbyters to the subordinate levites. Presbyters are 'of lower grade' and 'secondary dignity'. Thirdly, the preaching ministry of the priest is clearly signified in the paradigm of the disciples who were teachers of the faith (*doctores fidei*) and who, in his providence, Christ associated with the apostles as 'secondary preachers.' Because of the continuing importance of this prayer in Christian belief, teaching, and practice, it is here reproduced in full according to the reconstruction of H. B. Porter.

O Lord, Holy Father, Almighty, Everlasting God, bestower of all the honours and of all the worthy ranks which do thee service, thou through whom all things make increase, through whom everything is made firm; by the ever-extended increase to the benefits of rational nature by a succession arranged in due order; whence the priestly ranks and the offices of the Levites arose and were inaugurated with mystical symbols. Thus when thou didst set up high priests to rule over thy people, thou didst choose men of a lesser order and secondary dignity to be their companions and to help them in their labour. Likewise in the desert thou didst spread out the Spirit of Moses through the minds of seventy wise men, so that he, using them as helpers among the people, governed with ease countless multitudes. Likewise also thou didst impart unto Eleazar and Ithamar, the sons of Aaron, the richness of their father's plenty, so that the benefit of priests might be sufficient for the salutary sacrifices and the rites of a more frequent worship. And also by providence, O Lord, thou didst add, to the Apostles of thy Son teachers of the faith as companions, and they filled the whole world with these secondary preachers.

Wherefore, we beseech thee, O Lord, to grant these assistants to our weakness also, for we who are so much frailer need so many more. Grant, we beseech thee, O Father, the dignity of the presbytery unto these thy servants. Renew in their inward parts the Spirit of holiness (*ibid.*, pp. 25-27).

The Gallican Rite

Ordination prayers were prepared for the northern peoples in the sixth century. Before long these prayers were combined with those of the Roman rite. Nevertheless we may reconstruct the early Gallican rite from an eight-century version called the *Missale Francorum* and from the eighth-century Gelasian Sacramentary and its various recensions. The Gallican rite reflects a somewhat different perspective on the ministry from that embodied in the Roman rite. But like Roman, Anglican, and Orthodox rites today the different perspectives are complementary rather than conflicting.

The Gallican rite introduces to the west preliminary exhortations by the bishop to the assembled people, who are consulted about the candidate for the presbyterate. In Gaul they were expected to affirm the bishop's choice by acclamation. Another innovation is the anointing of the priest's hands.

The ordination rite for a presbyter is divided into four parts: the preliminary exhortation, a bidding, the prayer of consecration, and the anointing. The presbyter's preaching role is explicit. He is ordained as a residential officer who assists God's people to deepen their understanding of the faith.

In the exhortation the bishop appears as the leader of the wider community, the captain of the ship (*rector navis*) who wishes to consult his people about his choice for their priest. The priest is portrayed as a less hieratic figure than his Roman brothers. There is less notice of his dignity, rank, grade, and honour.

> Nor is it in vain that we recall the ordinance of the Fathers that the people also be consulted concerning the choice of those who are appointed to the regulation of the altar, since concerning his activity and present conversation what is sometimes unknown to most people is known to a few, and it is certain that anyone will more readily yield obedience to the ordained man for whom one hath given consent when he was being ordained... And so we ask your counsel concerning what you may know concerning his actions and conduct, of what you may judge concerning his merit with God as witness (*ibid.* p.49).

In the bidding prayer the priest is seen as an instrument for salvation who enjoys not only the blessing of the presbyterate but also the sacerdotal gifts of the Holy Spirit. The prayer in effect petitions for an abiding transformation of the man chosen for the office of salvation.

> Let us pray together, brethren, that this man, who is chosen to aid and further your salvation, may by the mercy of divine assistance secure the blessing of the presbyterate, in order that he may obtain by the privilege of virtue the sacerdotal gifts of the Holy Ghost, so that he be not found wanting in his office (*ibid.* p.51).

The consecration emphasizes the priest's service of preaching and demonstrates the inseparable connection between preaching in the wide and strict sense. The priest's preaching depends on his *believing* what he *reads*. This belief is the gift of grace but clearly it demands prayer, method, and industry in the recipient. Moreover, he is to be an *example* of that which he understands, believes, and teaches.

> Do Thou, O Lord, spread forth the hand of thy blessing upon this thy servant, N., whom we set apart with the honour of the presbyterate; so that he may show himself to be an elder by the dignity of his acts and the righteousness of his life, taught by those instruc-

tions which Paul presented to Titus and Timothy; that meditating day and night upon Thy Law, O Thou Almighthy, what he readeth he may believe; what he believeth he may teach; what he teacheth, he may practice. May he show in himself justice, loyalty, mercy, bravery; may he provide the example and demonstrate the exhortation, in order that he may keep the gift of thy ministry pure and untainted; and with the consent of thy people may he transform, by an untainted benediction, the body and blood of thy Son... (*ibid.*).

There are two prayers for anointing. The rite itself and the thrust of the first prayer are probably indebted to Roman Britain. In the Saxon Church anointing symbolized consecration and sanctification. According to the Anglo-Saxon Chronicle, King Guthrum of the Danes was anointed at his baptism. The fillet was removed some days later.

The King Guthrum came to him, one of thirty of the most honourable men in the host, at Aller which is near Athelney, where the King stood sponsor to him at baptism; and the ceremony of the removal of the baptismal fillet took place at Wedmore, and he was twelve days with the King...

The first Gallican prayer for the anointing of a priest prays that his hands may be consecrated and sanctified. The alternative prayer alludes to the Old Testament anointing of David as prophet and king. Anointing therefore also signifies the priest's ministry of the word. 'May these hands be anointed with hallowed oil and the charism of holiness. As Samuel anointed David to be a king and prophet, so be they anointed and perfected...'

The combined Roman and Gallican rites reflected by their complementary perspectives the Catholicity of belief and practice in Christian ministry. The Roman priest appears as a more hieratic and elevated officer while in Gaul he is portrayed more clearly as a servant of the people. In both perspectives, however, the priest is ordained to assist the bishop who is high priest and captain of the ship. In both rites the priest is ordained to preach in the strict and wide sense.

The early conflation of the Roman and Gallican rites formed the basis for the accepted Catholic ordination rite. Some changes were introduced in the middle ages and, as we shall see, continue to be made today. But with the composition of the Pontifical of William Durand in the thirteenth century the Roman rite was substantially established.

Late in the thirteenth century Bishop William Durand inserted three additions into the ordination rite for a priest. The Roman Pontifical, as modified by Durand, includes an allocution by the bishop *to the ordinands,* a profession of the Creed by the newly ordained, and a second anointing symbolizing the power to forgive sins.

Durand's allocution is concerned with preaching. Earlier in his Pontifical Durand has a directive which gives reason to believe there was widespread ignorance among 'the seven orders of clerics' about the duties of their offices.

> In the conferring of any order the pontifex should preach to the ordinands in his presence, for the sake of the simple, what order they are about to receive... Moreover, after ordination he should admonish the ordained and instruct them how they ought to live and serve God in their order and know what pertains to that order (William Durand, *Le Pontifical Romain du haut Moyen Age,* M. Andrieu, ed., Rome 1940, p. 360).

In another book the *Rationale,* Durand enumerates the fundamental knowledge a presbyter should command for effective preaching. The *Rationale* requires knowledge of the Roman missal, the readings, the antiphonal, the rite for baptism, the legislation for penance, the manner of computing liturgical feasts, and the collections of homilies to be read in church – hardly a theological armoury for the preacher. We observe, however, that the whole educational level of the faithful was low in an age when detailed medieval glass windows provided for many the primary 'book' of the epoch.

The allocution which inaugurates the ordination ceremony exhorts presbyters to assume responsibility for preaching and example. The pertinent passages, rich with instructions for preaching are as follows.

> My brother to be consecrated to the office of presbyter, strive to accept it worthily and, once accepted, fulfil it admirably. For it is the duty of a priest to offer, to

bless, to preside, to preach, and to baptize... You are consigned to the office of the seventy elders if through the sevenfold Spirit you observe the decalogue and are proved and mature in knowledge and deed. Under the same mystery and in the same figure, in the New Testament Our Lord chose seventy two disciples and sent them in pairs to preach that they might teach in both word and deed... May the fragrance of your life be a delight to the Church of Christ, that by preaching and example you may build up the house that is the family of God (*ibid.* p. 62).

Durand's second addition is equally significant for the preaching ministry of priests. The public profession of the Creed by the newly ordained signifies their new mission as preachers of the gospel. 'Standing in front of the altar in the presence of the bishop, let them profess the faith which they are to preach, saying "I believe in One God, etc." '

With the two additions we have discussed and that of a second anointing the Roman ordination rite was transmitted to the modern age.

The Friar Preachers

When Durand's Pontifical was put in use the primary preachers were bishops and priests with the care of souls. Occasionally monks were licensed to preach within monasteries, at monastic cathedrals and at synods. But preaching by monks was an exception. In 1277 Archbishop Pecham, himself a Franciscan friar, forbade Benedictine monks to attend universities, to engage in protracted studies or to shorten the office. Preaching by monks was never widespread in the middle ages although by the late fourteenth century a few monks, including Carthusians, enjoyed benefices.

Preaching by laymen was discouraged. A late medieval tract encouraged laymen to preach in the wide sense but to leave preaching in the stric: sense to priests.

If thou be a priest, and have knowledge and authority, preach and teach God's word to his people; and if thou be no priest nor clerk, but one of the people, then busy yourself on the holy day to hear preaching of God's word, and be about with thy good speaking and striving to bring thy neighbours to better living.

54

The quality of preaching by seculars was not always statisfactory. Master Rypon correctly said that poor preaching by priests led to confusion in the Church. 'If each churchman had the knowledge appropriate to his rank, then there would not spring up so many errors in the Church as spring forth these days.'

In general most seculars were average men who did their best to pass the torch of Christianity to their flocks. Priests are ordinary men reflecting the people from whom they come. That not all preaching by seculars was deficient seems clear from Chaucer's description of the 'pore parson'.

A holy-minded man of good renown
There was and poor, the parson in a town.
Yet he was rich in holy thought and work,
He was also a learned man, a clerk
Who truly knew Christ's gospel and would preach it
Devotedly to the parishoners and keep it (*The Canterbury Tales,* N. Coghill ed. and trans., Baltimore 1958, p. 30).

The disciplined order of Dominic was founded by an Augustinian canon who feared that neither seculars nor monks were capable of dealing with heresy. Dominic was a cleric at the age of 15 and a priest at 24. Impressed by the challenge of heresy and the difficulties of parish priests he grouped his first companions around him in the midst of the Albigensian heresy at Languedoc in 1205. He died at 52, two years after his order had assumed its substantial shape. The Dominicans were approved by Honorius III in 1216 as 'future fighters of the faith and true light of the world.' Their primary task, as their consitutions clearly affirmed, was preaching and salvation: 'our order is especially known from the beginning to have been instituted for preaching and the salvation of souls.' They were influenced by the Augustinian canons, by Prémontré and Citeaux. But, unlike the monks, they were not burdened with the administration of vast property. Their constitutions were brilliant, innovative, and participative, combining a genius for organization with the goal of universal salvation.

Significantly, in 1228 a general chapter decreed that no Dominican was to preach in public until he had studied theology for at least three years. As David Knowles remarks, 'For the Dominicans the defence and preaching of Catholic truth was an essential part of their life, the *raison d'être* of their order, and to this all other employments were sacrificed and subordinated.' Their constitutions state that 'all hours in the church should be recited briefly and succinctly lest study be impeded.' Study itself was a means to preaching. The Dominicans sought to reach men's minds – and to this end they studied scripture, the great commentaries, Hebrew, and even Aramaic.

Candidates were examined for knowledge as well as virtue. There was a theologian in every Dominican convent, several theologians at designated regional schools, and a *studium generale* for young friars at the great universities. The Dominicans soon established themselves at Paris, Oxford, Bologna, Montpellier, Cologne and Cambridge. By 1235 there were 120 Dominicans at the University of Paris.

The friars brought excitement to the universities and introduced their student colleagues to the fascinating study that is theology. Scholars were attracted to the order because the friars studied not with the vision of a comfortable career but with the ideal of informed preaching and the salvation of souls, the conversion of heretics and Saracens, the instruction of the unlearned. This ideal and the excellence of its practitioners attracted hundreds of talented undergraduates to the friaries. Moreover, with the arrival of Albert and Thomas Aquinas at Paris the Dominicans became custodians of the preaching ideal *and* a systematic metaphysics.

In the thirteenth century the learned Dominicans brought new life to the parishes. The friars demonstrated the vital role universities could play in the deepening of Christianity, they provided a wide network of schools and a creative way of life for the thousands of young men who joined them. They inspired priests to continuing education in theology and improved preaching. They brought with them a distinctive genius for communicating the good news that God was involved with all men and not just with the mighty. The Carmelite and Austin friars followed the lead of the Dominicans in making preaching the central mission of the mendicant priest.

Also in the thirteenth century there suddenly appeared in Dominic's Mediterranean country another young man with a unique grace from God, a vision, and a dream of evangelical poverty that was destined to haunt his followers to the present day. At Assisi in Umbria Francis, the wealthy son of a merchant, grasped in his intuitive way the need for better preaching if men were to really live the gospel life and reconcile themselves with the redeemed universe of sun and earth and birds and trees. Francis's distinctive way of uncompromising imitation of the poor (and therefore free!) Christ differed from the way of Dominic and that of almost everyone else before or since. But the two orders of friars were to interact and influence each other, with the Dominicans taking on something of Francis's kenotic poverty and the Franciscans, after much soul-searching, embracing Dominic's instinct for study and learned preaching.

Francis's dream was simple, universal, and in its impracticality incredibly practical. 'I say to you truthfully that Our Lord chose and sent the friars for the salvation of all the men in this world.' Francis's great heart embraced all men from the Sultan to the leper – and he himself personally preached Christ to the leper and Sultan. The way to save all men was evangelical preaching – in the wide sense of uncompromising imitation of Christ and in the strict sense of the spoken word of repentance. The first Franciscans fanned out in small bands to preach the word in poverty and total mobility. They were active missionaries who nonetheless acknowledged the necessity of prayer and periodic seclusion. Not all the friars, including Francis himself, were priests. In his final Testament Francis revealed his own concept of the priesthood and his determination never to preach in a parish without the permission of the pastor.

> Even though I had all the wisdom of Solomon, if I should find poor secular priests, I would not preach in their parishes without their consent... I will not consider their sins, for in them I see the Son of God and they are my Lords. I do this because here below I see nothing, I perceive nothing corporally of the most high Son of God, if not His most holy Body and Blood, which they receive and they alone distribute to others (Quoted in Paul Sabastien, *St. Francis of Assisi*, N.Y. 1917, pp. 337-8).

By 1223 they were a religious order. Their constitutions, promulgated in 1223, were not really as Francis had wanted them. The totality of evangelical poverty in imitation of Christ had been mitigated. Francis had hoped his friars would convert the world primarily through preaching in the wide sense of witnessing to Christ's poverty. Such an order could have endured – as so many religious orders could authentically endure – only if it were limited to a small number of men who shared the dedication of their founder.

The vocation of Francis, which he wished to transmit to his friars, had been to poverty, simplicity, and complete renunciation of the security that comes from ownership and position. Stripped of all, naked following the naked Christ, he might then call others to a change of heart by example rather than by words, and by direct appeal rather than by formal preaching and dispute. Himself a deacon only, he continued to the end to regard his friars as a body distinct from, and more lowly than, the priesthood; clerics and laymen were on an equality among them, and it was his desire that some should live in lowly hermitages, in unbroken prayer and praise, while others preached, and that all should in a measure share the lives of Martha and Mary (David Knowles, *The Religious Orders in England,* London, 1948, Vol. I, pp. 175-176).

In 1224 the friars crossed the Channel to England. The Oxford Greyfriars convent became a famous Franciscan house; and by 1240, at the height of their effectiveness, the Franciscans were internationally famous as a learned order. The lament of Brother Giles – 'Paris, Paris, thou hast destroyed Assisi' – was not altogether false.

As the Fanciscans grew as a clerical, priestly, and learned order they built convents, including stone convents, and bought books. From 1240–1246 Haymo of Faversham, the first English General, guided the growing order still further into the reaches of theological learning and informed preaching and teaching. By mid-century most Franciscans were priests.

In 1257 the great Bonaventure, as Minister General, exhorted the order to supplement wherever necessary the deficiencies of secular preaching. Bonaventure laboured for the establishment of large stone convents, for the use but not ownership of books, and for the displacement of manual work by the more exigitive labor of study in preparation for preaching.

In Bonaventure's mind, lay always the conviction that the chief task of the friars was to preach, and you cannot preach unless you first learn what to preach. If the friars were to be trusted to preach the truth, then they must be taught; they must spend many years in study; and they must have books to read and quiet places in which to read them (J. R. H. Moorman,

A History of the Franciscan Order, Oxford, 1968, p.
14).

And skilled preachers the friars were. They carried the
word, in proclamation and catachesis, to Islam, the Mon-
gols, Palestine, Syria, and North Africa. But it was in the
European villages that they excelled. Some indication of the
fervent content of their preaching is still reflected in contemporary historical reports, in homiletic manuals, and in
extant sermons. The friars excelled at preaching repentance
and redemption. An extant collection of illustrations compiled by friars for their own men, the *Liber Exemplorum,*
contains 213 examples pertaining to morals and doctrine, all
related to texts of scripture. The friars did not aim at mere
edification – their sermons stressed *action.*

Inevitably friction developed between the friars and some
bishops and seculars. Eventually, in 1300, Boniface VIII in
Super Cathedram ruled that mendicants could not preach in
their own church except at certain times and that they needed the permission of bishop and pastors to preach in secular
pulpits. This was reinvoked by Clement V in 1311.

The friars felt the scorn of Langland in *Piers Ploughman*
and of Chaucer in *The Canterbury Tales.* They were accused of pendantry, avarice, and even immorality. Chaucer's Wife of Bath feared not spirits but friars hiding in the
hedges. But it was John Wyclif who, after his break with
the friars over the primacy and the Eucharist, accused them
bitterly of seducing villagers from the parish priest. Thus
Wyclif:

> They do not fear to shape their sermons by formal ar-
> rangement of the subject matter and other foolish de-
> vices, which they do to please the people. And thus...
> they make people think that sermons are nothing ex-
> cept in their form and thus they prevent simple
> priests so that they do not dare to preach to the peo-
> ple (*The English Works of John Wyclif hitherto un-
> printed,* F. D. Matthew, ed., London, 1880, p. 445).

Such criticisms were extreme and, at least for the majority
of the friars, unfair. But the fact remains that the friars rapidly reached a peak – even more rapidly than most religious
Orders – and then declined. They became learned, famous,
comfortable, and sometimes lax. They quarrelled with each
other, with the seculars, and even among themselves. How
fast and far the mendicant Orders declined is sadly illustrated in the event that by 1500, after decades of unseemly

strife, the Franciscans were split into Conventuals and Observants. The Conventuals pleaded their obedience to the Pope; the Observants pleaded their freedom from ownership. But with notable exceptions the evangelical fire of Francis had burned low. How fast and far the Dominicans had declined is illustrated by the event that in 1518 the Order that Dominic had gathered to champion the faith was exalting and defending John Tetzel in the fateful dispute over the sale of indulgences.

When the magisterial reformers appeared in the sixteenth century preaching by some regulars and seculars was informed and inspiring. But many priests, including manor and chantry priests, were considered adequate merely because they offered sacrifice, administered the sacraments and on occasion gave rudimentary sermons. No longer were the early sons of Dominic and Francis on hand to inspire villagers, at green and church, with their sermons.

The reformers put great stress on the preaching ministry. In response Catholic apologetics emphasized the priest's role at the Eucharist. The Council of Trent, in its reform of seminaries, did lay the groundwork for better informed seculars, but the Council gave scant inspiration to priests to look upon informed preaching as their primary task.

CHAPTER IV

PREACHING IN THE MODERN AGE

The friars – despite their loyalty to the papacy and their steadfast defence of the Catholic Mass – were in one important respect precursors of the reformers. Wyclif, Hus, the Lollards and the magisterial reformers all shared the friars' conviction that dedicated preaching was the minister's paramount mission. Owen Chadwick writes:

> The reformers, reacting against salvation by forms or by ritual, saw the sacraments as one part, though a momentary and indispensable part, of a total ministry to the people, wherein the supreme and ultimate act was the exposition of the word of God (*The Reformation,* Baltimore, 1966, p.60).

At Wittenberg the prolific author, scholar, and reformer, Martin Luther, taught that men were justified by faith in Jesus Christ. But justifying faith was itself dependent on informed preaching of the good news. Luther argued that all baptized Christians, and especially appointed ministers, were consecrated and commissioned to preach the gospel to all men. The word drew men to the Church, preserved the Church, and ruled the Church. As James Atkinson says:

> ... the word of God came to occupy the central place in Luther's mind. He saw the Church's chief mission as the preaching of the word rather than the administration of the sacraments, for the word not only gave the Church her commission but preserved and governed it (James Atkinson, *Martin Luther and the Birth of Protestantism,* Baltimore 1968, p.84).

In 1523 Luther revised the Lord's Supper for the evangelical communities at Wittenberg. While his *Formula of the Mass* is a revision of ancient Catholic usages, its controlling principle, like that of subsequent evangelical liturgies, is the centrality of the word. Luther eliminated the offertory and canon – and placed the sermon at the center of his liturgy: –

Introit
Kyrie

Gloria
Salutation
Collect
Epistle
Gradual
Gospel
Creed
Sermon
Preface
Consecration
Lord's Prayer
Communion
Agnus Dei
Alleluia
Blessing

Three years later, in 1526, Luther composed a vernacular folk Mass for the German people. Once again the sermon was central. It was Luther's dream that a return to the Bible would result in better-informed preachers. He envisaged small communities gathered for Bible reading, prayer, a homily, the Eucharist, and conversation. His simplified *German Mass* proceeded as follows:

Hymn or Psalm
Kyrie
Collect
Epistle
Hymn
Gospel
Creed
Sermon on the Gospel
Lord's Prayer in paraphrase
Blessing and administration of bread
Sanctus and Elevation
Blessing and administration of cup
Hymn
Agnus Dei
Collect and Blessing

Luther contended that every parish should enjoy – and support – a trained and dedicated minister. If, due to age or ignorance, ministers were incompetent to preach but were nonetheless virtuous men, they should read the gospel and a printed homily. However, the Wittenberg reformer soon learned to his sorrow that even in reformed Churches learned and virtuous pastors were not easy to find. At Luther's own Wittenberg, Pastor Bugenhagen preached faithfully four times a week – but men of his calibre were in short supply.

The Augsburg Confession of 1530, an important Lutheran statement, illustrates the German reformers' emphasis on biblical learning, biblical preaching and biblical correction by appointed ministers. The bishop was not commissioned to 'interfere in civil government' but:

> to preach the gospel, to remit and retain sins, and to administer sacraments... to discern doctrine, to reject doctrines contrary to the gospel, and to exclude from the communion of the Church wicked men whose wickedness is known, and this without human force, simply by the Word (*ibid.* p. 290).

Luther's colleague, Philip Melanchthon, contended that the prerogative of the bishop was to preach. The German reformers went so far as to teach that an 'ordained' man who ceased preaching was no longer a bishop or minister. Thus Melanchthon:

> Preaching the gospel is so peculiarly the prerogative of a bishop that it is not proper to substitute another for him, to teach in his place. If, therefore, he do not teach, he is not a bishop.

The Swiss reformers acknowledged the teaching of German Protestants that justification was not by 'works' but by faith in Christ. The minister was not commissioned for the 'work' of a propitiatory sacrifice – but to preach the word in sermon and sacrament. The Geneva reformer, John Calvin, stressed the importance of preaching and sacraments.

> As to applying to us the merit of his death, that we may perceive the benefit of it, that is done not in the way in which the Popish Church has supposed, but when we receive the message of the gospel, according as it is testified to us by the ministers whom God has appointed as his ambassadors, and is sealed by the sacrament.

In his monumental *Institutes of the Christian Religion* Calvin argued that the particular functions of pastors were to preach, in public and private, and to administer the sacraments.

> We may infer that in the office of the pastors also there are these two particular functions: to proclaim the gospel and to administer the sacraments. The

manner of teaching not only consists in public discourses, but also has to do with private admonitions (IV, III, 6).

The reformed Swiss tradition was influential in Britain. All the leading English reformers emphasized the ministry of preaching. Thomas Cranmer, in his first and cautious Communion Service of 1549, clearly imparted renewed emphasis on preaching in his petition for bishops, pastors, and curates.

> Geue grace (o heauenly father) to all Bishoppes, Pastors, and Curates, that thei maie bothe by their life and their doctrine, set furthe thy true and liuely worde, and rightely and duely administer thy holy sacramentes (Edward P. Echlin, *The Anglican Eucharist in Ecumenical Perspective*, Seabury Press, N.Y., 1968, p.29).

In 1552 Cranmer, significantly, left this petition intact although he suppressed or radically altered other petitions in the prayer for the Church. The priest was 'ministre of God's worde'; the Lord's Supper a remembrance of Christ's sacrifice; the offering 'of ourselves, our souls and bodies', our praise and thanksgiving.

Cranmer provided written exhortations and homilies, for unlettered pastors, to be read at regular intervals and (at the suggestion of Martin Bucer) to be read unexpurgated from beginning to end.

The 23rd Anglican Article asserts that ministers are appointed for public preaching and administration of the sacraments; there is no explicit mention of sacrifice. It was this same emphasis on word and sacrament in the Anglican Ordinals of 1550 and 1552, when conjoined with deliberate suppressions of references to sacrificial priesthood, that induced Rome to withhold recognition of the validity of ministers ordained with the revised Ordinal.

> It is not lawful for any man to take upon him the office of public preaching, or ministering the Sacraments in the congregation, before he be lawfully called and sent to execute the same. And those we ought to judge lawfully called and sent which be chosen and called to this work by men who have public authority given unto them in the Congregation, to call and send Ministers into the Lord's vineyard.

The English reformers most influenced by the teaching of Calvin, Zwingli, Bucer and Bullinger argued that a minister of the gospel must be a disciplined, informed servant of the

64

word. The fiery John Hooper of Gloucester pointedly demanded a ministry 'whose mind and soul be instructed and furnished with godly doctrine, and a fervent zeal and spirit to teach his audience, to establish them in the truth, and to exhort them.' As for the Lord's Supper, 'the more simple it is the better it is and the nearer unto the institution of Christ and his apostles.'

Both on the continent and in Britain Catholic reformers who remained in communion with the historic Church also championed a revival in preaching. The ministerial strife of the sixteenth century (and thereafter) focused on sacrifice. Catholic bishops and theologians had no quarrel with Protestants on the importance of preaching. Reginald Pole, a legate at Trent and later a papal representative in the Marian interlude, exhorted Catholic priests to take their preaching ministry seriously.

> The duty of preaching will be fulfilled satisfactorily if exercised not only by public preaching, but also privately. The pastor will call to himself those of his flock whom he knows to have wandered from right faith or good morals, and he will try by teaching, admonishing, exhorting, and if necessary by deterring, to lead them again to Catholic faith and good morals.

As the reformation gathered momentum and as the counter-reformation took hold there was a noticeable improvement in ministerial preaching – but not enough to satisfy either Rome or the reformers. Luther bitterly indicted the ignorance and laxity of many evangelical ministers. And Rome decided to reform the training of clerics. Owen Chadwick describes the situation well.

> In general, there was less graft, less corruption, less illegality, less non-residence, less simony, and there was more teaching, more preaching, more pastoral care, better education, better understanding of the faith by laymen, less wordliness and more fervour among pastors or priests, less superstition and more religion, less arid intellectualism, and a more Biblical apprehension (Owen Chadwick, *The Reformation*, p.406).

Most of the improvement stemmed from better preaching. In reformed England, Scotland, Switzerland, and Germany, but also in northern Italy and wherever the Jesuits were operative, ministry of the word was improving. However, in parts of southern Italy, Germany and France Catholic preaching remained intolerably deficient. Some ignorant men, both Catholic and reformed, were still being ordained; others were ordained merely to administer sacraments and read the prescribed gospel and homily.

In general preaching improved more rapidly in the cities than in the country. Sermons were provided almost daily at Wittenberg, Strasburg, Torgau, and Rostock. Hour (and half-hour!) glasses began to appear on the proliferating pulpits. Catechisms – long, short, and medium – and vernacular Bibles were widely available. Reading desks made their appearance at the east end of churches until, in his canons of 1604, James I made them mandatory for all English churches.

The Council of Trent

The Fathers who convened in the southern Alps in 1547 were faced with a surplus of beneficed priests. In fact the benefice system was a major attraction to hirelings who became clerics without theological formation or dedication to the word. One council father remarked that 'there seem to be so many uneducated and ignorant priests that their number is almost infinite.' Unfortunately Trent, while its reforms were to be extensive, was not prepared to uproot the benefice system completely. Referring to this entanglement with benefices, a Spanish Dominican, Martin de Mendoza, predicted that 'the Church will not be truly reformed until it consists of few and poor members.'

The council promptly set out to reformulate the accepted Catholic faith in the priesthood and to reform the clergy. At the outset of the debates preparatory to a dogmatic decree on priesthood the question of preaching was raised. Since the reformers had stressed the ministry of the word, should the council in its dogmatic statement include preaching as a priestly power? Or should it confine its decree to defence of doctrines seemingly denied by Protestants?

A council at Cologne in 1536 in the heart of Protestant territory had confronted the same question. Cologne had responded by emphasizing preaching as the primary priestly office – and in so doing had emphasized what the reformers also stressed.

The office of priests consists primarily in preaching the word, then in confecting the body and blood of our Lord and administering the other sacraments..., finally in praying for the whole Church and the prosperity of the Christian people.

At Bologna in 1547 it seemed the Council of Trent was going to acknowledge preaching as a priestly office. A draft decree prepared by the Tridentine theologians condemned the proposition that the ministry could be *reduced* to preaching – but it acknowledged that preaching was a priestly power. The draft canon which condemned the false proposition included the following qualification: 'nevertheless priests should accurately preach the word of God to their people and provide the food of sound and salutary doctrine.' But this qualification was dropped. After years of intermittent debate on the priesthood a drafting commission in October 1562, endorsed the proposition that a priest who did not preach was still a priest, but the proposition was preceded by a qualification similar to the discarded one of 1547: 'although it is not denied that ministry of the word pertains to priests, nevertheless they do not cease to be priests if they do not exercise this office.' In late October, 1562, the Augustinian General and legate, Seripando, amended the text even more positively: 'although it is certain and not to be doubted that ministry of the word pertains to priests, nevertheless they do not cease to be priests if because of a just impediment they do not exercise this office.' In the final decree the entire qualification was omitted – probably for the sake of brevity and because the Roman curia and the council wished to concentrate on truths denied by the reformers (Henri Denis, 'La Thélogie du presbytérat de Trente a Vatican II', in *Vatican II, Les Prêtres*, J. Frisque and Y. Congar, eds. Cerf, Paris, 1968, pp. 205-208).

The dogmatic decrees on priesthood were the outcome of almost two decades of debate, conducted intermittently from 1546 to 1563. Trent's point of departure was the sacrificial nature of the Eucharist and the sacrificial role of the presbyter-priests of the new covenant. Other ministerial powers such as ministry of the word (and the priesthood of the laity) were not emphasized. Nevertheless the Fathers recognized the importance of preaching in the drafts, debates, and decrees of the council.

The reforming decree of 1563 instructed bishops to provide substitutes for unworthy rectors: 'The bishops, as the delegates of the Apostolic See, may depute to the said illiterate and unskilled rectors, if they be otherwise of a blameless life, temporary coadjutors or vicars...' Moreover, preaching was a prime reason for the reform of absenteeism – 'preaching of the divine word' made residency of the pastor imperative.

When the Fathers discussed priestly formation there was a surprising amount of controversy. Some Fathers argued that if standards were set too high the Church would be deprived of the sacramental ministry of many ignorant but devout men. The Archbishop of Bassano testified that he 'had known such men, who celebrated with such devotion that their prayers were undoubtedly more acceptable to God than those of many fine preachers.' Originally a draft canon had required that subdeacons should be 'instructed in letters and those things which pertain to the order to be exercised.' Later this was amended to require deacons to be able to preach (*praedicare*). James Laynez, the Jesuit General who had argued for a compulsory moral training of seminarians, was vehemently opposed to this particular requirement. 'The devil induces the legislation of those things which destroy the priesthood under pretext that a deacon should preach and other things of this kind.' So many Fathers voted *'non placet'* that the preaching requirement for deacons was dropped. Nevertheless, the final draft of 1563 made it abundantly clear that ordinands were to understand at least 'those things necessary for salvation.' Deacons promoted to the priesthood were first 'proved to be, by a careful previous examination, capable of teaching the people those things which it is necessary for all to know unto salvation.'

Trent most effectively provided for better preaching – in the wide as well as in the strict sense – by its famous legislation for the establishment of seminaries in every part of the Church. Students were to be instructed by beneficed teachers. Where these were unavailable or inadequate the bishop would provide a substitute. The academic curriculum would be such that future Catholic priests would receive a broad humanistic and theological education.

> They shall learn grammar, singing, ecclesiastical computation, and the other liberal arts; they shall be instructed in sacred Scripture; ecclesiastical works; the homilies of the saints, the manner of administering the sacraments, especially those things which shall seem adapted to enable them to hear confessions; and the forms of the rites and ceremonies (*The Canons*

and Decrees of the Council of Trent, J. Waterworth, ed., London 1848, pp. 188-189).

The council also legislated for preaching in its decree on the sacrifice of the Mass.

> The holy Synod charges pastors and all who have the care of souls, that they frequently, during the sacrifice of the mass, expound, either by themselves or others, some portion of those things which are read at Mass, and that amongst the rest, they explain some mystery of this most holy sacrifice, especially on the Lord's day. (ibid., p.191).

It is noteworthy that in its initial reforming decree in 1546 the council had stressed preaching as the bishop's primary task – a ministry which he shared with those who had the care of souls. And in the closing days of the council, in its penultimate reforming decree in November, 1563, the council reiterated this same teaching – which was to be taken up yet again, and refocused, by Vatican II.

> The holy Synod, desirous that the office of preaching, which peculiarly belongs to bishops, may be exercised as frequently as possible, for the welfare of the faithful... [Bishops] shall themselves in person, each in its own Church, announce the sacred scripture and the divine law or, if lawfully hindered, it shall be done by those whom they shall appoint to the office of preaching; and in the other Churches by parish priests, or if they be hindered, by others to be deputed by the bishop... (ibid. p.200).

Trent reasserted the visible, hierarchical, permanent, and sacrificial nature of the priesthood – which the continental reformers denied. The council acknowledged but did not emphasize the priest's ministry of the word.

Preaching in the Counter-Reformation

The gradual implementation by Catholic dioceses of Trent's reforming decrees resulted in better-informed priests, better preaching, and, therefore, better-instructed laymen. However, Christendom was now indefinitely divided. Different traditions with different emphases went their own ways without sharing their different patrimonies. The fragmentation of God's people was an impoverishment which affected the quality of preaching. Catholic preachers in the long counter-reformation epoch – which continued almost until Vatican II – often emphasized the divergent doctrines and practices which divided Catholics from their separated brethren. Nor was scripture given adequate attention in the seminaries. 'Scriptura sola' had been the Protestant battlecry. In reaction Catholics tended to emphasize the teaching in ecclesiastical tradition.

Post-Tridentine theology focused not on the bishop but on the priest; and within this focus it concentrated on the priest's role at Mass. As a result priests tended to look upon themselves – and be looked upon – as adequately fulfilling their mission if they offered sacrifice, presided at the sacraments, and administered parishes. Their intellectual formation was often narrow, legalistic, parochial, polemical, non-biblical, and in a word 'scholastic'. The Church historian Michael Gannon notes that by the nineteenth century,

> ... the intellectualism in which they were formed and which they themselves evidenced was such as to restrict rather than expand the mind, to seek simple preservation and elaboration of antique truths rather than their creative development; to promote a defensive style of apologetics rather than open historical criticism; to build fences instead of bridges. It was an intellectualism fairly bristling with non-intellectualism, and its name was 'scholasticism' – not that neo-scholasticism which was fostered in the Thomistic revival of Pope Leo XIII, nor that academic neo-scholasticism which even today commands the respect of protestant and secular scholars in the Medieval Academy of America and elsewhere, but that artificial, gerrymandering scholasticism, composed of syllogism piled Ossa on Pelion, frozen into textbook form, and memorized by unnumbered seminarians (Report to American Bishops, April 1971).

The Code of Canon Law, promulgated in 1917, required sufficient doctrine and good morals in those licensed to preach. Presumably the 'sufficient' doctrine was imparted in the seminary.

The ordinary preachers were priests and deacons. The laity, including religious, were expressly forbidden to preach. Women, therefore, were excluded from ministry of the word in church.

> The Ordinary of a place or religious superior is gravely bound in conscience not to give the faculty or li-

cence to preach to anyone unless it is first clear that he has good morals and sufficient doctrine... (CIC 1340,1).

The faculty of preaching should be given only to priests or deacons, not however to other clerics unless for a reasonable cause and in exceptional cases the Ordinary shall judge otherwise. All the laity, including religious, are forbidden to preach in church (CIC 1342).

The Code provided for sermons on Sundays and holy days and more frequently during Lent and Advent. But a fateful exceptive clause was inserted: 'The Ordinary may permit the sermon to be omitted on the more solemn feasts and even, for a just cause, on Sunday's (CIC 1344,3). Unfortunately many bishops extended the 'just cause' beyond all reason. In *lieu* of a homily or sermon many captive audiences were forced to hear letters from the Chancery – sometimes several Sundays a month – requesting funds or discussing trivia. The excessive resort by some bishops to the exceptive clause was a deplorable abuse.

The Code also provided for the subject-matter of sermons, namely, 'a brief explanation of the gospel or some part of Christian doctrine' (CIC 1345). The compilers of the Code seemingly had in mind rudimentary sermons. 'In sermons those things should be explicitly expounded which the faithful should believe and do for salvation' (CIC 1347,1).

The 1917 Code, therefore, envisaged communities of 'faithful' who required instruction in the essentials necessary for salvation. Except for the occasional visiting missionary their preacher was the pastor with care of their souls. Neither seminary formation, the quality of preaching, nor the legislation for preaching were adequate to the emerging laymen of the twentieth century.

Compounding the difficulty was a *surplus* of seminaries. When almost every diocese felt obliged to staff its own seminary the result was an overextension of limited theological and pedagogical talent. Pope Pius XI was aware of the deficiency and on several occasions called for an amalgamation of smaller seminaries. On his golden jubilee as a priest the Pope issued an encyclical on priesthood in which he urged regional bishops to 'concentrate and unite their forces in a common seminary, fully worthy of its high purpose... Often in fact we have suggested and recommended them.' But this wise counsel was not everywhere heeded. For example the United States, which in 1900 had 109 seminaries, found itself by January I, 1960 struggling to staff and support 525, most of which were mediocre and many of which one decade later were empty shells, hotels, schools, retreat-houses and office buildings.

But the most serious and durable obstacle to the effective ministry of preaching, especially in 'developing' consumer societies, was the urge to activism which took priests away from serious prayer, continuing study, and dedicated preparation of sermons. On the eve of the council God's people were demanding more and better preaching than they had experienced. But priests, in addition to being inadequately trained in theological method, were engulfed by Circean blandishments of administrative and social activism. Fortunately a majority of the Fathers who convened at Vatican II were determined from the outset to promote a more comprehensive teaching on the ministry than the defensive teaching of Trent. The old polemics were receding and the Fathers were able to teach that preaching – in word, liturgy and life – was the priest's paramount mission.

Vatican II

Vatican II's teaching on the priesthood is indeed global and comprehensive. The council recalls the unique high priesthood of Christ who was consecrated and sent by his Father. The baptized and confirmed people of God participate in Christ's consecration and mission. As a priestly people they proclaim the wondrous deeds of God and join the sacrifices of their holy lives to Christ's unrepeatable and continuing sacrifice. Within the priestly people bishops and priests share publicly in Christ's priesthood. Through the sacrament of Holy Orders they are configured to Christ as head. The consecration and mission of the apostles is therefore handed down in a particular way to bishops who in turn share their priesthood with presbyter-priests.

Unlike Trent the Vatican council does not focus its teaching on priests of the second rank. Its teaching centres on the bishops, who through their consecration and communion with the episcopal college and its head enjoy the fullness of sacramental priesthood. Priests, who share this priesthood in a lesser degree, are co-operators of the episcopal order.

Their mission is to proclaim the gospel, to gather men to the Church, to teach God's people to unite their spiritual sacrifices with Christ's sacrifice, to lead them to the sacramental sacrifice of the Eucharist, and to go forth with them from the Eucharist to reconcile the world.

From this concise recapitulation of the council's teaching we can observe how central to the priest's mission is the ministry of preaching. In all the documents which touch on the priesthood – the Constitution on the Liturgy, the Dogmatic Constitution on the Church, the Decree on the Bishop's Pastoral Office, the Decree on priestly Formation and, finally, the Decree on the Ministry and Life of Priests – the council affirms that the priest's mission is to preach, sanctify, and lead, *in that order*. In the quieter atmosphere of the ecumenical age the Fathers felt free to state unambiguously that preaching was central to the priest's mission, a mission which derived from and reached its apex in the Eucharist which is itself the great proclamation of the Trinitarian act in Christ. This teaching is of course continuous with that of Trent. But it is a development nonetheless and a great shift in emphasis.

We have noticed that priests, as co-operators with the order of bishops, have as their principal office the mission of preaching. In its first constitution, that on the liturgy, Vatican II reminded God's people that preaching comprehends both proclamation and teaching. The priest therefore preaches to lost sheep outside the fold as well as to his many brethren within. The Church's preaching builds up God's people as the light of the world.

> Therefore the Church announces the good tidings of salvation to those who do not believe, so that all men may know the true God and Jesus Christ whom He has sent, and may repent and mend their ways (cf. Jn 17.3; Lk 24.27; Acts 2.38). To believers also the Church must ever preach faith and repentance. She must prepare them for the sacraments, teach them to observe all that Christ has commanded (cf. Mt 28.20), and win them to all the works of charity, piety, and the apostolate. For all these activities make it clear that Christ's faithful, though not of this world, are the light of the world and give glory to the Father in the sight of men (Decree on the Liturgy, n. 9).

The central document of the council, the Dogmatic Constitution on the Church, which was finally promulgated in

1964, enumerates the duties of a bishop under the following three heads – prophetic, cultic, and royal. At the beginning of its description of a bishop's duties the document says that preaching occupies an 'eminent' place. Bishops proclaim to outsiders and bring them to the faith, they teach their brethren, and they correct errors. Since priests in their own degree share in the bishop's responsibilities it is worth noting the council's emphasis on episcopal preaching.

> Among the principal duties of bishops, the preaching of the gospel occupies an eminent place. For bishops are preachers of the faith who lead new disciples to Christ. They are authentic teachers, that is, teachers endowed with the authority of Christ, who preach to the people committed to them the faith they must believe and put into practice. By the light of the Holy Spirit, they make that faith clear, bringing forth from the treasury of revelation new things and old (cf. Mt. 13.52), making faith bear fruit and vigilantly warding off any errors which threaten their flock (cf. 2 Tim. 4.1-4) (n. 25).

The Decree on Priestly Formation describes the purpose of seminary training under the familiar three heads and in the same order – preaching, sanctifying, leading. Seminarians are asked to study God's word, to savour it through meditation, and to learn how to communicate it in word and deed. They are to familiarise themselves with the Fathers, the liturgies, the official teachings of the Church, and the writings of theologians. The council implies that seminarians are to acquire a methodology for a lifetime of continuing education in Christianity. This document – which has not been everywhere followed by seminary officials – treats the priest's eminent duty of preaching with the utmost seriousness. A profound knowledge and prayerful experience of scripture are especially desirable.

> Let these students, then be readied for the ministry of the word, so that they may always grow in their understanding of God's revealed word, may know how to grasp it through meditation, and express it through word and conduct (n. 4).

But a question remains – why did the council put preaching in the first place? Was this a historically conditioned emphasis similar to Trent's emphasis on cult? In other words is there something theologically permanent, something in the historic reality of Christian ministry that justifies this emphasis? Or, considering the Church's freedom to restructure its ministry, is the pre-eminence given to preaching an internal reordering to meet current needs?

It seems that the primacy of preaching is grounded in the very reality of Christian ministry, that this pre-eminence is no mere adjustment to circumstances but an inspired intuition by Vatican II into the profound reality of Christian ministry, and that whenever priests and people put preaching in a secondary place (after cultic or leadership or activist roles) there will follow, even if the de-emphasis is temporarily necessary, an amount of confusion within the Church. Whenever the priest's preaching role is slighted it is imperative for the Church to reasses its origins and its history as well as its present experience. This is what Vatican II did – and its documents pervasively teach the primacy of preaching. Aloys Grillmeier addresses himself to the *raison d'être* for the priority given to preaching; his reflections concur with our own. Christianity is the religon of God's self-disclosure; salvation begins and continues with the word of God's revelation.

> The parallelism between episcopal and priestly tasks is also valid for the order in which they are enumerated; the preaching of the good news is put in the first place. From the point of view of history of religon, precedence might well have been given to the cultic function, which is in fact emphasized. But the preaching of the message is rightly put first, because salvation begins with the word of God's revelation. What primarily specifies the Christian religion is that it is the religion of the full self-disclosure of God in Christ. The preaching of the word comes first in the celebration of the liturgy and in the missions, the Church addressing believers in the former and unbelievers in the latter (Aloys Grillmeier, 'The Hierarchical Structure of the Church with Special Reference to the Episcopate,' in *Commentary on the Documents of Vatican II*, H. Vorgrimler, ed., N.Y. 1968, Vol I, p. 22).

At the close of the council there was promulgated a special decree on the priesthood. This decree had a turbulent history. In the second session, in 1963, several fathers objected that the Constitution on the Church did not treat the priesthood adequately. At the session's close a special message to the priests of the world was circulated – and rejected as inadequate. In the third session, in 1964, a list of propositions on the priesthood was circulated – and despite the pressures of time and work referred back to committee for revision. In the fourth session, in 1965, a detailed decree was circulated, debated, modified, passed, and promulgated on 7 December, 1965. The decree summarizes and develops earlier conciliar statements on the priesthood. The priest has as his 'primary duty' the proclamation of the gospel.

The People of God finds its unity first of all through the Word of the living God, which is quite properly sought from the lips of priests. Since no one can be saved who has not first believed, priests, as co-workers with their bishops, have as their primary duty the proclamation of the gospel of God to all. In this way they fulfill the Lord's command: 'Go into the whole world and preach the gospel to every creature' (Mk 16.15). Thus they establish and build up the People of God.

For through the saving Word the spark of faith is struck in the hearts of unbelievers, and fed in the hearts of the faithful. By this faith the community of the faithful begins and grows. As the Apostle says: "Faith depends on hearing and hearing on the word of Christ" (Rom 10.17) (n.4).

The preaching office comprehends both proclamation and teaching. Instruction in the fundamentals is especially appropriate at the Eucharist.

The ministry of the Word is carried out in many ways, according to the various needs of those who hear and the special gifts of those who preach. In areas or communities which are non-Christian, the gospel message draws men to faith and the sacraments of salvation. In the Christian community itself, especially among those who seem to understand or believe little of what they practise, the preaching of the Word is needed for the very administration of the sacraments. For these are sacraments of faith, and faith is born of the Word and nourished by it. Such is especially true of the Liturgy of the Word during the celebration of Mass. In this celebration, the proclamation of the death and resurrection of the Lord in inseparably joined to the response of the people who hear, and to the very offering whereby Christ ratified the New Testament in his blood (n. 4).

76

Preaching demands a lifetime of preparation. Because every priest serves the people of a particular time and place with historically conditioned problems the priest's proclamation does not take place in an ivory tower. His mission is to apply the gospel to the time and place with which he is engaged. His preparation therefore includes a keen sensitivity to the joys, sorrows, and questions of the people he serves.

> No doubt, priestly preaching is often very difficult in the circumstances of the modern world. If it is to influence the mind of the listener more fruitfully, such preaching must not present God's Word in a general and abstract fashion only, but it must apply the perennial truth of the gospel to the concrete circumstances of life. (n. 4).

Informed preaching requires unrelenting application to prayer, the study of scripture and theology, familiarity with the 'concrete circumstances of life', and the clear formulation of the Christian message. The council reminds priests that preaching unites not only their hearers but even themselves to Christ. For it is the grace of God and not native talent, eloquence, nor even disciplined application to service of the word that moves the hearts of men.

> As priests search for a better way to share with others the fruits of their own contemplation, they will win a deeper understanding of 'the unfathomable riches of Christ' (Eph. 3.8) as well as the manifold wisdom of God. Remembering that it is the Lord who opens hearts and that sublime utterance comes not from themselves but from God's power, in the very act of preaching his word they will be united more closely with Christ the Teacher and be led by his Spirit (n. 13).

The priest, configured to Christ as head, gathers and unites God's people through his preaching. But preaching is effective only when the priest unites Christians at the Eucharist, the sacrament of unity. At this point the council touches on something of paramount importance for the identity of the contemporary priest and for the welfare of all the men in the world. The priest's role, the source of his identity and personal value in the community, is to be the primary preacher in the local community, to unite men in the Eucharist, and through his preaching to inspire all men with the unfathomable riches of the gospel – so that not just priests but the whole people of God will go forth from the

Eucharist as a reconciling community. As the Church struggles to break out of isolation and effectively serve mankind, the council reminds God's people that mere 'Massgoing' is not enough. Inspired by the preaching of their priests, God's people are united in the Eucharist as the goal of preaching – but also as a beginning of their mission which is to bring eucharistic love to the world, to reconcile divided mankind with itself and with its environment.

The council affirms the connection between preaching, Eucharist, and service of the world. If any one of these three – preaching, Eucharist, service – is missing, then Christianity is ineffective and incomplete. Informed preaching by priests, which culminates in the eucharistic mission to mankind, is mandatory for the self-understanding and reconciling mission of the Church.

> No Christian community, however, can be built up unless it has its basis and centre in the celebration of the most Holy Eucharist. Here, therefore, all education in the spirit of community must originate. If this celebration is to be sincere and thorough, it must lead to various works of charity and mutual help, as well as to missionary activity and to different forms of Christian witness (n. 6).

Since the promulgation of the Decree on the Ministry and Life of Priests the Church has been reordering and refocusing its ministry. Deacons have returned to serve as intermediaries between the Church and the world and to perform many services which previously withdrew the priest from effective preaching. God's people are deepening their understanding of Christian ministry. In the recently revised ordination rite for priests there has been included a homily stressing the priest's participation in the consecration and mission of Christ. The ordination prayer still derives from the ancient Verona rite – but a significant addition reflects the renewed understanding that bishops and priests are, before all else, servants of the word of the gospel.

> May they be worthy co-operators of our order, so that the word of the gospel may reach to the ends of the earth; and all the nations, gathered together in Christ, may be transformed into the one holy people of God.

CHAPTER V

EPILOGUE: THE FUTURE PRIEST AS PREACHER

The famous Little Prince of Antoine St. Exupéry learned in his voyage to planet earth that 'one takes the risk of weeping a little when one lets oneself be tamed.' The theologian learns that he takes the risk of being misunderstood when he emphasizes one aspect of a mystery.

The priesthood is a great mystery – and we have emphasized the aspect of preaching. Yet there are other aspects and, therefore, other emphases. Tridentine theology emphasized the priest's role at the Eucharist. Recent Catholic theology has emphasized the priest's share in Christ's kingship, his role as leader. Some theologians even go beyond the traditional tripartite division – prophetic, priestly, royal – and emphasize the priest's role as centre of unity in local communities.

These emphases, and many more, are not contradictory but complementary. Dialectically they interact in such a way as to illuminate with the light of Christ the mystery of priesthood. Nevertheless our thesis is that the priest is the primary preacher in a local community and that preaching in his paramount service. We contend that the emphasis of Vatican II on the priest as preacher is grounded in the historic reality of Christian priesthood.

Moreover, the council's methodology, which puts the priest's prophetic role in first place, coincides with the contemporary yearning of God's people for better-informed preaching. The yearning of the laity for better ministry of the word than they have experienced may in fact be the prompting of the Spirit to lead the Church out of its present crisis in the ministry. In the voices of God's people the Spirit discloses his presence – and the current demand for informed preaching should be carefully discerned. Young and old, progressive and traditionalist, rich and poor – all voice dissatisfaction with this lifegiving ministry. The widespread dissatisfaction indicts sermons (and religious education) mediated in neo-scholastic, text-book, juridical, and catechism categories. God's people demand informed preaching solidly founded on God's revelation in Christ, which proclaims the gospel and provides instruction in concepts and symbols appropriate to the modern, changing, historical world in which Catholics seek salvation and reconciliation.

This does not imply that only 'traditionalist' preaching is today scored as inadequate. There are criticisms voiced, especially by educated laymen, about preaching devoted almost exclusively to foreign affairs and social controversies. God's people require and even demand guidance in applying the gospel to the piercing problems of today; but many indict sermons based almost exclusively on current events. They sense that only if they are thoroughly conversant with God's word in Christ through the ministry of their pastors will they appropriate and live their Christianity. Only if their ministers of the word truly mediate the gospel to them will they, God's priestly people, go forth to heal society.

It is embarrassingly trite to say that there is widespread confusion in the historic Church of Rome in the wake of the post-war theological revival and its fruition at Vatican II. It is less trite, however, to suggest that the pervasive disillusionment with Catholic preaching, which we have just described, may point to the main source of the confusion now in the Church. The widespread dissatisfaction with ministerial preaching should be carefully discerned.

The process of discernment, here as always, requires indifference to one's own comfort and openness to the Spirit. Where informed preaching is lacking, all God's people, and not just priests, must do whatever is demanded, including financial sacrifice, that the word of God may properly inspire God's people. If married priests, for example, are forthcoming, they must be financially supported so that they can devote their energies to service of the word.

Renewed dedication to the ministry of preaching will revolutionize the lifestyle of many priests. Activism, whether administrative or social, must be only a small part of the priest's routine. He cannot, in all honesty, preach the word of God with boldness if preaching is only a minor concern in his life. On the contrary his whole life – in pulpit, liturgy, and leadership – must be informed preaching. There will be informed preaching (by priests) only if there are informed priests. And there will be informed priests only if priests devote their lives to service of the word. The priest cannot respond to the yearnings of God's people if he spends his midweek in the deadly routine of activism.

The priest's mission demands awareness of the needs, concerns, yearnings, questions and anxieties of contemporary society. For he gathers and unifies the Church, leads God's people to the Eucharist, and from the Eucharist guides them – through the word – in their outgoing mission to the world. But if he himself spends too much time in direct and immediate involvement with society's enormous problems he will be unable to provide informed preaching in the strict sense. Here again we recall the openness to the Spirit that careful discernment demands. How can the priest do the most good? By social work, or by disciplined prayer, study, preparation, and meditation on the word?

We repeat our thesis that the priest is the primary, albeit not the only, preacher in a community and preaching is his paramount service. We should add however that the orientation of some seminaries seems to be pointed in another direction. If seminarians spend at most eight months a year at school; if their extensive vacations are devoted mainly to work and 'apostolates'; if even during their months at the seminary their weekends are frequently spent in work or travel; if their midweek courses are something less than a demanding foundational methodology for a lifetime of service of the word; then, how can we expect young priests to provide the informed service of the word for which God's people are yearning? It is perhaps significant that some clerical religious orders whose scholastics until recently spent eleven months a year in exigitive preparation for the ministry now permit students to take to the road whenever classes are recessed for a few days. It may be, as one sympathetic Protestant observer has warned, that we are preparing not lifelong ministers of the word but social workers for the early seventies.

For men already ordained the pressures to withdraw from prayer, study and thorough preparation of preaching are enormous. Improved financial circumstances, insurance, opportunity to travel, colour TV, stereo, comfortable cars, the pressures of administration, committees and of course the fashionable idea that the social barricades are where the priest's action is – these pressures have proved anything but conducive to ministry of the word. Many priests now recognize this and have turned their unprecedented mobility into valuable channels such as the organization of houses of prayer, weeks of renewal and institutes in continuing education for priests.

The present situation, therefore, seems to come down to something like this. On the one hand, God's people are demanding better and more professional ministry of the word; on the other, despite hopeful signs such as those just noted, seminarians and priests are engulfed by blandishments of activism.

As one suggestion in the current dialogue within Catholicism on the role of the priest I propose that within very few years deacons and laymen should administer Catholic parishes. They are competent to assume responsibility for the 'many things' hitherto too absorptive of the priest's time, including parish organizations, rudimentary religious instruction, preparation of catechumens and financial affairs. Lay men and women can and should provide such services as distribution of the Eucharist, social work, involvement in politics, civil rights and peace movements. In regions where permanent deacons are available they can provide such services as officiating at wakes and burials, devotions, marriages, visiting and anointing the sick, viaticum, and baptism.

This proposal, at least on the surface, is anything but original. It has an all-too-familiar ring. It is in fact the very proposal, voiced by many laymen and within the heart of the priest, that has contributed to the widely recognized 'identity-crisis' of today's priest. Many Catholics feel that this proposal relegates the priest to presidency at the Eucharist and penance.

But this brings me back to my thesis. What is overlooked in too much of the discussion of priesthood is the priest's service of the word. Priests may have gone all the way around the world to find what they sought was in their own rectory. In the almost audible groanings of the priest, as the laity assume his former functions, the Spirit may be speaking to God's people.

There may be a convergence in the priest's search for identity and the laity's yearning for better ministry of the word. Identity is the role assigned to a man in a society, the role expected of him, the role from which he derives his lifegiving sense of personal value. While priests seek identity, layman seek informed ministry of the word. If priests do not proclaim the gospel, who will build community through service of the word? We suggest that priests can find their identity as stewards of the good news in a Church that hungers for this service as rarely before. While there are lay-

82

men who have stopped going to Church and laymen who feel the Church is moving too fast, there are also laymen like those described by Martin Work. We have all met them – and I submit that their suffering could be healed by priests dedicated to the service of preaching.

> They see nothing but churning and change, stop and go, milling and disorder. Old ideas, programs and structures seem to be crumbling under attack. No adequate substitutes have yet clearly surfaced to attract them to a new and better commitment. In the meantime, their old commitment keeps them attached to the Church and its institutions – but the old fire is burning low and could well suffocate ('A Report on the Laity', *The Catholic Mind*, February 1971, p. 41).

In exceptional exigencies the priest himself will necessarily engage in administration, politics, agriculture, medicine and social work. Nevertheless if the emerging laity and deacons liberate the priests from these tasks he will be free to deepen his experience of scripture and theology so that he can inspire *many* Christians to human and cosmic reconciliation. Informed preaching by full-time servants of the word can attract the laity to what Martin Work calls 'a new and better commitment.'

Other priests serve as ministers of the word through specialized scholarship. By bringing the gospel to bear on man's most profound probings priest-scholars facilitate the union of faith with science. Priest-economists, for example, can mediate the word to laymen such as Julius Nyerere of Tanzania, and Eduardo Frei of Chile, who seek a new and human economy, based not on competition-acquisitition-consumption but on the gospel of human brotherhood. Priest-scientists, by proclaiming that all reality is dear and redeemed, facilitate reconciliation of science and technology with the redeemed earth. Priest-theologians provide an essential service to bishops, priests, deacons and all God's people by explaining and reinterpreting the faith. An important service of the priest-theologian is to mediate the results of his scholarship to his brother priests through lectures, homily-outlines, and articles for priest's journals.

If Catholic priests discover their identity as disciplined ministers of the word the potential of Christianity as a leaven of reconciliation is enormous. Christians have not always been a reconciling community because they have not always understood the real meaning of their commitment. And they have not understood their commitment because informed preaching was wanting. Ghandi observed that the only fault with Christianity was Christians. And Avery Dulles has written,

> ... the churchgoing public does not always appear as a radiant sign of hope. Christians, like other men, seem to be primarily concerned for those things which, in the words of Jesus, the heathen seek (Avery Dulles, *The Survival of Dogma*, N.Y. 1971, p.74).

The failure of the churchgoing public to witness to Christian hope is obvious to anyone who has seen consumer-oriented Christians competing on the parking-lot after Mass. It is less obvious to suggest that a shallow 'Mass-going' Christianity is the legacy of shallow preaching. Over forty years ago Pope Pius XI proclaimed clearly:

> Each one, therefore, must receive his due share, and the distribution of created goods must be brought into conformity with the demands of the common welfare or social justice. For every sincere observer is conscious that, on account of the vast difference between the few who hold excessive wealth and the many who live in destitution, the distribution of wealth is to-day gravely defective (*Quadragesimo Anno*, in *Church and State Through the Centuries*, Sydney Ehler and John Morall eds., London 1954, p. 430).

Yet how many priests appropriated this message – which is nothing more than a contemporary application of the gospel? How many preached this? How many really studied and meditated on the social encyclicals? How many by their attachment to 'the motor car' and the consumer society which produced it preached quite another message? The fact is that many Christians are still collaborating with consumer societies that seek 'multiplication of products', 'profit', 'domination', and exploit men 'from whatever part of the world'. As these words are written ten per cent of humanity (the developed consumer societies) consume fifty per cent of the earth's resources. These same industrialized societies, having ravaged their own environments, are now attempting through advertising and economic imperialism to impose urbanized industrialization on the third world.

We submit that a fateful failure in Christianity has been the refusal of Christians to understand and proclaim the full meaning of the redemption. In Christ man *and the earth* are redeemed, in Christ man and nature are as brothers, in Christ man shares with and does not plunder the earth, in Christ nature too groans in expectation of the final redemption of men, of new heavens and a new earth.

The post-war ravishment of the American landscape is antithetical to the gospel of redemption. Sadder still is the current savaging of England and Ireland, much smaller countries and trustees of a culture, a history, a way of life. Informed – and uncompromising – discernment of these signs of the times and preaching of the wider meaning of the redemption can (and must) inspire Christians to drop the tools of destruction, to share the earth with other men, to share themselves with a sibling earth. In 1971 Auxiliary Bishop Thomas Gumbleton, of Detroit, called upon his brother bishops whose 'eminent' duty is preaching the gospel to challenge Christians to question the consumer society.

> I hope that the Bishops will challenge their people, especially those of the rich nations, to question the 'Consumer Society' with its definition of human development solely in terms of material acquisitions that provide convenience, comfort and luxury ('Thomas Gumbleton', *America*, Sept. 25 1971, p. 203).

This is indeed a challenge to Christians in consumer societies, many of whom readily reply *'Mater si, magistra non'* whenever the teaching office proposes sharing based on the gospel. Bishops and priests should take up Gumbleton's challenge – which is the challenge of universal redemption – and preach it from the housetops. Not only developed nations need preaching of the wider meaning of the redemption; there are many Christians in the third world who seek 'wealth' not in sharing but (as American advertising teaches) in Americanization.

That God created, loves, and redeemed the earth is clear from Genesis, the prophets and psalms, the gospels, SS John and Paul, and from the unbroken, though often ignored, stream of Christian teaching that extends from the earliest Christian communities to Chesterton and Teilhard. It is a corollary to our thesis that when informed priests provide informed preaching about the fullness of the redemption, then and only then will a significant number of Christians go forth from the Eucharist to actively reconcile redeemed man with the redeemed earth. Through informed preaching of the redemption Christians will experience their Saviour's love for the earth and all created things. 'Look at the birds of the air; they do not sow and reap and store in barns; yet your heavenly Father feeds them' (Mt 6.25-29). How often Christ refers to God as 'your', 'our' Father. Christians are to address God as Father. But to relate to God as a Father is to imitate God, to take on God's mannerisms, to be like God, in a word, to be God-imitators. And God the Father whom Christians imitate shares and loves and reverences the earth. Even the birds on the air he feeds. Moreover, God who is Father of men is also Father of the birds. Man and nature are as brothers. To Jesus himself even the wind was as a sibling. 'The wind blows when it wills; You hear the sound of it, but you do not know where it comes from or where it is going' (Jn 3.8).

Those commissioned to preach in Christian assemblies are empowered to inspire their fellow Christians with the wider meaning of the redemption, to challenge men to seek a humane form of economy, a new attitude towards 'wealth', a new kind of sharing with all men and with the earth, a new brotherhood of redeemed men with each other and with the earth which shares the same heavenly Father. Vatican II proclaims to all men:

> We humbly and ardently call for all men to work along with us in building up a more just and brotherly city in this world. We call not only upon our brothers with whom we serve as shepherds, but also upon all our brother Christians, and all men of good will ... For this is the divine plan, that through love God's kingdom may already shine out on earth in some fashion as a preview of God's eternal kingdom. ("Message to Humanity," in *Documents of Vatican II*, p. 6).

It is significant that six years after the council the bishops at the 1971 synod of bishops in extensive deliberations focused on and combined two aspects of Christianity, the same two aspects upon which we have focused and which we have combined in this epilogue: Catholic priesthood and human reconciliation. The synod recognized that informed preaching of Catholic priests is necessary if God's priestly people are to be a reconciling community.

In conclusion, the future priest as preacher must respond to Simeone Weil's pointed question – 'How can the Church call itself Catholic when the universe itself is left out?' The priest must refocus the gospel and proclaim what has been slighted for centuries – the universal redemption. He must challenge men, including his fellow Christians and brother priests, who band with the spirit of destruction. When Alfred fought for the Wessex vines destruction came through the iron fist of the Dane. Today it comes through the iron wheel of unbridled technology which, having laid waste weald and down, rolls greedily towards Severn side and the faint green hills of the west.

> For our God hath blessed creation,
> Calling it good. I know
> What spirit with whom you blindly band
> Hath blessed destruction with his hand.
> Yet by God's death the stars shall stand
> And the small apples grow
>
> *The Ballad of the White Horse* by G. K. Chesterton

Bibliography

I General

C. K. Barrett, *Biblical Problems and Biblical Preaching*, Philadelphia, 1964.

M. Bourke, 'The Catholic Priest: Man of God for Others', *Worship*, Vol. 43, no. 2, pp. 68-79.

A. Church, *The Theology of the Word of God*, No. 12 of Theology Today Series, 1970.

E. P. Echlin, *The Deacon in the Church: Past and Future*, N.Y., 1971.

R. H. Fuller, *What is Liturgical Preaching?*, London, 1960.

E. Haensli, 'Preaching', *Sacramentum Mundi*, ed. K. Rahner, N.Y., 1970, Vol. V, pp. 81-88.

H. Kung, *The Church*, London, 1967.

J. J. Von Allmen, *Preaching and Congregation*, Richmond, 1963.

II Special

Chapter I

C. K. Barrett, *The First Epistle to the Corinthians*, N.Y. 1968.

M. Bourke, 'Reflections On Church Order in the New Testament', *The Catholic Biblical Quarterly*, Vol. XXX, No. 4, pp. 493-511.

R. A. Brown, *Priest and Bishop*, N.Y. 1970.

E. Kasemann, *Essays On New Testament Themes*, London, 1964.

J. N. D. Kelly, *The Pastoral Epistles*, N.Y. 1963.

E. Schweizer, *Church Order in the New Testament*, London, 1960.

Chapter II

J. P. Audet, *La Didachè*, Paris, 1958.

H. Chadwick, *The Early Church*, London, 1967.

R. H. Connolly, *Didascalia Apostolorum*, Oxford, 1969.

J. Daniélou, *Origen,* London, 1955.

G. Dix, *The Apostolic Tradition of Hippolytus* 2nd ed., London, 1968.

Eusebius, *The History of the Church From Christ to Constantine,* ed. G. A. Williamson, London, 1965.

K. Lake, *The Apostolic Fathers,* 2 Vols., N.Y., 1919.

M. Staniforth, *Early Christian Writings,* Baltimore, 1968.

Chapter III

J. Cooper, *The Testament of Our Lord,* Edinburgh, 1902.

J. Gaudemet, *L'Eglise dans L'Empire Romain,* Paris, 1958.

D. Knowles, *The Religious Orders in England,* 2 Vols., Cambridge, 1948.

J. R. H. Moorman, *A History of the Franciscans,* London, 1968.

C. Munier, *Les Statuta Ecclesiae Antiqua,* Paris, 1960.

G. R. Owst, *Preaching in Medieval England,* Cambridge, 1926.

H. B. Porter, Jr., *The Ordination Prayers of the Ancient Western Churches,* London, 1967.

D. N. Power, *Ministers of Christ and His Church,* London, 1967.

R. W. Southern, *Western Society and the Church in the Middle Ages,* London, 1970.

Chapter IV

J. Atkinson, *Martin Luther and the Birth of Protestantism,* London, 1968.

O. Chadwick, *The Reformation,* Baltimore, 1966.

E. P. Echlin, *The Anglican Eucharist in Ecumenical Perspective, Doctrine and Rite from Cranmer to Seabury,* N.Y., 1968.

J. Fresque and Y. Congar, eds., *Vatican II: Les Pretres,* Paris, 1967.

J. Guryot, ed., *The Sacrament of Holy Orders,* London, 1962.

H. Jedin, *A History of the Council of Trent,* 2 Vols., St Louis, 1961.

J. T. McNeill, *The History and Character of Calvinism,* London, 1954.

H. Vorgrimler, ed., *Commentary On the Documents of Vatican II,* 5 Vols., N.Y., 1967.

J. Waterworth, *The Canons and Decrees of the Council of Trent,* London, 1848.

Chapter V

H. Barnette, *The Church and the Ecological Crisis*, Grand Rapids, 1972.

R. A. McCormick, 'Towards An Ethics of Ecology', *Theological Studies,* Vol. XXXII, no. 1, pp. 97-107.

J. J. Megivern, 'Ecology and the Bible', *Ecumenist,* Vol. 8, no. 1, pp. 69-71.

P. Ramsay, *Fabricated Man,* New Haven, 1970.

H. P. Santimire, 'Ecology and Schizophrenia: Historical Dimensions of the American Crisis', *Dialog,* Vol. IX, no. 1, pp. 175-192.

J. Sittler, 'Ecological Commitment as Theological Responsibility', *IDOC*, Sept. 12, 1970, pp. 75-85.

INDEX

Aaron, 48
Abyssinia, 45
Alexandria, 38, 39
Alfred, King, 52, 87
Ambrosiaster, 44
Antioch, 14
apostles, 12, 19, 26, 27
Aquinas, 56
Asia Minor, 28, 29, 32, 34, 45
Atkinson, James, 61
Augsburg Confession, 63

Barnabas, 12
Bassano, Archbishop of, 68
Bologna, 67
Bonaventure, 58
Boniface VIII, 59
Bucer, Martin, 64
Bugenhagen, 63
Bullinger, 64

Caesarea, 38, 39
Callistus, 34
Calvin, 63, 64
Celsus, 40
Chadwick, Owen, 65
Chaucer, 55
Chesterton, 85, 87
Citeaux, 55
Clement of Rome, 25, 26, 34
Clement V, 59
Code of Canon Law, 70, 71
Cologne, Council, 66
Constantine, 43
Corinth, 23, 25, 36
Cornelius, 15
Cranmer, 64
Crete, 20
Cyprian, 41, 42

David, King, 52
delegates, 20, 21
Demetrius of Alexandria, 38
Denis, Henri, 67
Didache, 27-29
Didascalia, 37, 38
Dominic, 55
Dulles, Avery, 84
Durand, William, 53, 54

Egypt, 34, 45
Ephesus, 20, 24
Ephiphanius, 30
Ethiopia, 34
Eusebius, 30, 34, 43
Ezekiel, 16

Francis St, 56-60
friars, 54-61

Galatians, 16, 17
Gallican Rite, 50-52
Gaul, 43, 46, 47, 50
Geneva, 63
Giles, Brother, 58
guardian-presbyters, 21-23
Gumbleton, Thomas, 85
Guthrum, King, 52

Haymo of Faversham, 58
Heraclas, 38
Hippolytus, 34, 35, 37, 38, 47
Honorius III, 55
Hooper, John, 65
Hus, 61

Ignatius of Antioch, 28-30
Irenaeus, 32, 33
Isidore of Seville, 44

27 THE THEOLOGY OF THE EUCHARIST
BY
JAMES QUINN, S.J.

The Eucharist is the Heart of the Christian life. It is the sacrament of Christ's presence because it is the sacrament of his sacrifice. It is the summary, the sign and the means of salvation.

In celebrating the Eucharist we stand before the Father in joyful praise of all his wonderful works. The presence of Christ, and our unity in him, enables us to offer to the Father perfect praise and thanksgiving. Christ himself the mighty act of God in history, the One whose body is the centre of the new liturgy in spirit and truth.

At the Eucharist Christ sends the Holy Spirit to build up the Church as his body and to make the world a temple to God's glory. The reconciling work of the Eucharist brings unity to creation.

The Eucharist prepares the Church on earth for the glory of heaven. It is the joyful sign of the second Coming of Christ. It is the beginning, the firstfruits, of the transfiguration of the material universe into a new world wholly dominated by the risen Christ.

43 ROMAN CATHOLICISM, CHRISTIANITY AND ANONYMOUS CHRISTIANITY
BY
J. P. KENNY, S.J.

The Church is mission. Proclaiming the good news is not a function accessory to her; rather it determines her essence. By definition, the Church is that gathering in the Spirit of the chosen people of God who provide the visible heralds of Christ. As 'the universal sacrament of salvation', the Church embodies God's constant offer of salvation to all men of all time. But if beyond the frontiers of the visible Church, Christ and his Spirit are already at work, why bother about the missions? What is their aim and meaning? If in fact a man can reach Christ and have his Spirit without the structures and paraphernalia of organized Christianity, why require him to submit to the Catholic Church, and what is the point of being a Christian at all? It is to be hoped that the ventilation of these questions, which concern all Christians and even all religious-minded men, may be enlightening, stimulating and comforting.

46 THE CHURCH AND THE WORLD
BY
RODGER CHARLES, S.J.

The claim of the secularising theologians, or those who popularise what they say, is summed up by the statement of Bonhoeffer concerning the rejection of the religious premise and man's coming of age. In popular discussion, it seems to the author, this is taken to mean that by rejecting many of the external forms and the positive beliefs of Christianity man mysteriously becomes more Christian. But Christianity only had its impact on history because of those externals and beliefs, which were not contradictory to the spirit of Christ in the Church but a manifestation of it. Further, the very things which Western man is most proud of are a result of his Christian inheritance, an inheritance which he owes to the labours of traditional Christianity, strengthened and guided by its dogma, through hundreds of years. It is not secularisation which will save modern man from his present predicament. It is a return to and a strengthening of the values and the institutions of traditional Christianity.

15 WHY WERE THE GOSPELS WRITTEN?
BY
JOHN ASHTON, S.J.

For what we know of the life and teaching of Jesus we depend almost entirely upon the gospels, which are thus the fountainhead of Christian belief. But for nearly eighteen centuries no attempt was made to examine them critically, and when it eventually did come the onset of critical exegesis had devastating consequences.

It is only in the last few decades that the Catholic Church has managed to come to terms with the techniques of biblical scholarship elaborated over these two centuries. Having briefly expounded and assessed the new techniques and commenting upon the preoccupations of the scholars who have them, this book tries to take a fresh look at the gospel tradition itself and then to describe the contributions made to the tradition by the gospel writers themselves.

THEOLOGY TODAY SERIES
The titles published to date are:

First published in the Netherlands
Made and printed by Van Boekhoven-Bosch N.V., Utrecht